LEARNING HOW TO LEARN

Learning how to learn

JOSEPH D. NOVAK AND D. BOB GOWIN

Department of Education
New York State College of
Agriculture and Life Sciences
Cornell University

CAMBRIDGE
UNIVERSITY PRESS

PUBLISHED BY THE PRESS SYNDICATE OF THE UNIVERSITY OF CAMBRIDGE
The Pitt Building, Trumpington Street, Cambridge, United Kingdom

CAMBRIDGE UNIVERSITY PRESS
The Edinburgh Building, Cambridge CB2 2RU, UK
40 West 20th Street, New York, NY 10011-4211, USA
477 Williamstown Road, Port Melbourne, VIC 3207, Australia
Ruiz de Alarcón 13, 28014 Madrid, Spain
Dock House, The Waterfront, Cape Town 8001, South Africa

http://www.cambridge.org

First published 1984
Reprinted 1986 (twice), 1988, 1989, 1990, 1991, 1993 (twice),
1994, 1995, 1996, 1997, 1998, 1999, 2000, 2002 (twice)

Printed in the United States of America

Typeset in Galliard

A catalog record for this book is available from the British Library

Library of Congress Cataloging in Publication data is available

ISBN 0 521 31926-9 paperback

CONTENTS

v

Contents

Contents

FOREWORD

During the past year two aspects of my life have often been juxtaposed. As president of a national teaching association, I have served on state and national commissions concerned with clarifying the crises in science education and I have traveled the country discussing the identified crisis with classroom teachers. As a science educator concerned about how students, particularly female and minority students, learn, I have assessed and analyzed learning among black teenagers who used the constructs described within this book. What amazes me in retrospect is how and why those two activities were so separate, so distinct. Surely the first concern of the prestigious commissions and researchers, as well as the journalists who publicized their work, was how children learn. Yet neither in the headlines nor in the footnotes did I find references to meaningful learning – to education. Rather, I read about training, testing, disciplining, and employing. Yet, shouldn't the science education of the children in my research help them think about the consequences of using a nuclear weapon as well as teach them how to read the operational manual and run the machine?

As the hoopla concerning the crisis fades and the work of rejuvenating education begins, I suggest that parents, teachers, administrators, and researchers read this book. It succinctly and clearly presents a view, a theory, of how children learn and, therefore, how teachers and others can help children think about science as well as other topics. Its ideas and techniques may be adopted for preschoolers when objects are conceptually ordered, or for theoretical physicists when findings are conceptually organized. In addition, the authors offer evidence that their propositions work, that children can *learn how to learn*.

Two of the constructs described and discussed in the book, Concept and Vee diagramming, augment learning by combining the theoretical with the practical, the unfamiliar with the familiar. The third one, clinical interviews, allows teachers and parents to assess such integration. Together they build a firm foundation for learning and for thinking.

Perhaps times are changing. Recently I gave a workshop, mandated by a state's commission on education, for some rather reluctant science teachers. They were tired of unsolicited, external edicts about longer school days, fewer teacher aides, more student-centered laboratories, student and teacher competency tests, and differential teacher pay. Politely they listened to my summary of national reports; quietly they assessed texts with readability formulas; passively they evaluated computer software. But the atmosphere changed when I introduced concept mapping. Enthusiastically and eagerly, they sought more information on how children learn because they could relate the material to learning problems in their classrooms. I believe that changes will come not from legislators or commissioners, but from classroom teachers. Novak and Gowin relate learning with teaching in a way designed to help classroom teachers who, in turn, will educate our children.

Jane Butler Kahle

West Lafayette, Indiana

PREFACE

THIS BOOK was written for all those who believe that learning can be more effective than it now is, either in schools or in any other educational setting. The work grows out of sixty years of the authors' combined experience and research dealing with problems of educating in classroom and field settings.

For almost a century, students of education have suffered under the yoke of the behavioral psychologists, who see learning as synonymous with a *change in behavior*. We reject this view, and observe instead that learning by humans leads to a *change in the meaning of experience*. The fundamental question of this book is, How can we help individuals to reflect upon their experience and to construct new, more powerful meanings?

Furthermore, behavioral psychology, and much of currently popular "cognitive science," neglects the significance of feelings. Human experience involves not only thinking and acting but also feeling, and it is only when all three are considered together that individuals can be empowered to enrich the meaning of their experience. All readers of this book have surely experienced sometime during their schooling the debilitating effect of an experience that threatened their self-image, their sense that "I'm OK." We have found repeatedly in our research studies that educational practices that do not lead learners to grasp the meaning of the learning task usually fail to give them confidence in their abilities and do nothing to enhance their sense of mastery over events. Whereas *training* programs can lead to desired behaviors such as answering math problems or spelling correctly, *educational* programs should provide learners with the basis for understanding why and how new knowledge is related to what they already know and give them the affective assurance that they have the capability to use this new knowledge in new contexts. Schooling is too often an assault on students' egos because the rote, arbitrary,

verbatim instruction so common in classrooms has few intrinsic rewards. Students who do seek meaning in such instruction often fail.
For them, school is at best frustrating and at worst an ordeal in
which they must suffer the ridicule of teachers, classmates, and sometimes parents. We commonly blame these victims for failing at rote
learning, and categorize them as "learning disabled" or, more deni-
grating, school dropouts or simply losers. The cost of these failures,
both to the individuals and to society, is enormous.

We have come to recognize that questions of learning cannot be
addressed comprehensively unless we consider simultaneously questions dealing with three other commonplaces involved in education:
teachers and how they teach, the structure of the knowledge that
shapes the curriculum and how it is produced, and the social matrix,
or governance, of the educational setting. In any episode of educating, all four must be considered. The strategies we present are designed to enhance educating by helping learners to learn about human learning, about the nature of knowledge and the construction
of new knowledge, about strategies for better curriculum design,
and the possibilities for governance of education that is liberating
and empowering.

We do not intend to demean teachers. We seek instead to celebrate
the sense of achievement that results when students and teachers share
meanings and give emotional support to each other. The relationship between students and teachers need not be an adversarial one –
poor pedagogical practices or a poor curriculum, or both, are usually
to blame. Much that is wrong with education can be changed, and
most of the needed changes are not expensive. Although programs
that offer new pedagogical strategies or create new curricula do cost
money, it costs us very little to change our minds. Are our ideas cost
effective? We need only consider one point. Teachers have been
working very hard to achieve what is both impractical and burden-
some, and therefore costly: We have expected them to *cause* learning
in students, when of course learning must be *caused by* the learner.
When students learn about learning in the ways we recommend, they
take charge of their own learning. Relieved of the burden of having
to cause learning, teachers can concentrate on teaching. When the
goal of teaching becomes the achievement of shared meaning, a great
deal of both teachers' and students' energy is released. The strategies
offered in this book can not only help learners, they will also make
better and more powerful teachers. And therein lies much of the

potential of the book, for in the course of a career, a teacher can influence the lives of thousands.

There is, we believe, a solid theoretical foundation for the practical strategies we put forward. This is a "how to do it" book with a solid theoretical base and considerable empirical research behind its claims. Throughout the book, we cite our own and others' works, as well as the Master's and PhD theses of some of the more than fifty students who have worked with us. But we are not out to convince the skeptic. Rather, our purpose is to provide workable strategies to help students learn how to learn. We also illustrate how these same strategies can be applied to better organize educational programs and to benefit future research in education. We recognize that helping students learn how to learn in the sense we intend is a new and profoundly important endeavor. Because we have just begun to explore the human potential for learning, our ideas will undoubtedly be revised and expanded in the future. Our experience has shown us, however, that the basic strategies we propose are useful and powerful, and can only become more so as they evolve.

So we invite you, the reader, to join us in an adventure in education that is potentially revolutionary and has no limits, for there are no limits to the power of the human mind to construct new meanings from experience.

J. D. Novak
D. B. Gowin

Ithaca, New York
May 1984

ACKNOWLEDGMENTS

S IR ISAAC NEWTON said that if we achieve something of
value, it is because we stand on the shoulders of giants who have
come before us. We recognize our indebtedness to the brilliant thinkers
whose work has shaped our thinking, especially John Dewey, Joseph
Schwab, and David Ausubel. But equally important have been the
many graduate students and teachers who have worked with us, offered counsel and criticism, and often provided encouragement as
well as wisdom. Among the teachers are Mary Bente, Harris Brot-
man, Loy Crowder, Jay Decatur, Sarah De Franco, Richard Eklund,
Jon Glase, Kenneth Greisen, David Henderson, Roald Hoffmann,
Donald Holcomb, Jane Kahle, Doug Larison, James Maas, Richard
McNeil, James Noblitt, Walter Slatoff, and Charles Wilcox.

The students who have contributed directly to the ideas presented
in this book include Cheryl Achterberg, Mary Arnaudin, Julia Atkin,
Charles Ault, Benzy Bar Lavie, Stewart Bartow, Christopher Bogden, Michael Brody, Regina and Bernardo Buchweitz, Peter Cardemone, Hai Hsia Chen, Kathy Colling, John Cullen, Debra Dyason,
John Feldsine, Eugenia Francese, Patrick Galvin, Geri Gay, 'Laine
Gurley, Doreet Hopp, June Kinigstein, Susan Laird, Carlos Levan-
dowski, Susan Melby-Robb, Leah Minemier, Sister Mollura, Marli
and Marco Moreira, Brad Nadborne, Greg Norkus, Joseph Nussbaum, Terry Peard, Leon Pines, Richard Rowell, Judith and James
Stewart, Donna Talmage, John Volmink, Margaret Waterman, and
Linda Weaver.

Some of the research work that led to the development of the
strategies reported here was supported by funds from Shell Compa-
nies Foundation, Hatch Act grants, and the National Science Foundation (SED-78-116762). Art work was done by Julie Manners. We
are most grateful to Sid Doan and Alison Reissman, who typed numerous drafts of the manuscript.

LEARNING ABOUT LEARNING

WHAT IS THIS BOOK ALL ABOUT?

WE ARE CONCERNED with educating people and with helping people learn to educate themselves. We want to help people get better control over the meanings that shape their lives. Educating is powerfully liberating; failures in educating are powerfully oppressive. Wherever educating occurs, in schools and out, we think we can help people get better control over the events of educating, and thus over that part of their lives that is being transformed.

"Seek simplicity, but distrust it," claimed Alfred North Whitehead. We share this view, and desire in seeking simplicity to preserve complexity. Sometimes simple ideas are so obvious they are obscure. We will try to illustrate simple but potentially powerful strategies to help students learn and to help educators organize learning material. The two principal educational tools we will discuss are *concept mapping* (see Figure 1.1), which is a way to help students and educators see the *meanings* of learning materials, and *knowledge Vee diagramming* (see Figure 1.2), which is a way to help students and educators penetrate the *structure* and *meaning* of the knowledge they seek to understand. In addition, we will describe some strategies that help students and teachers move toward what we will call *shared* meanings and feelings. This task is ambitious, but our experiences have shown that it is not unattainable. We invite you to join us in an exploration that is still very much in progress, for we (the authors) and our students are continuing our search for ways to become better teachers and/or learners and to help students learn what it means to learn. This process is symbiotic: illuminated by the teacher and student sharing ideas and advanced by their mutual commitment to educating.

In Chapter 2, we will present a full discussion of concept mapping.

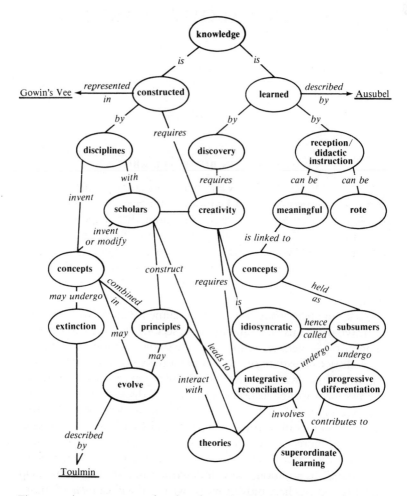

Figure 1.1 A concept map showing the major ideas presented in this book regarding acquisition and construction of knowledge. Key concepts are shown in ovals; appropriate linking words form key propositions.

We provide both practical advice and theoretical perspective, stressing that people think with concepts and that concept maps serve to externalize these concepts and improve their thinking. In Chapter 3, we show that Vee diagramming based on epistemological study of an event is a simple and flexible way to help students and teachers

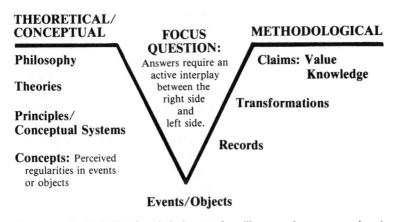

Figure 1.2 Gowin's Vee heuristic invented to illustrate the conceptual and methodological elements that interact in the process of knowledge construction or in the analysis of lectures or documents presenting knowledge.

grasp the structure of knowledge. It has been our experience that once people have tried applying concept mapping and Vee diagramming to familiar material, they see the value and power in these strategies.

For decades it has been debated whether education is an art or a science. We will not enter into this debate, which is somewhat analogous to the debate regarding heredity versus environment as the determinant of human performance. Whatever the detailed issues may have to say to us, our general premise is that education can be both an art (or craft) and a science and that human potential is influenced by both heredity and environment. Because almost no one today advocates eugenics, the only option available to educators is improvement of the learning environment. The strategies presented in this book are based on and derived from theoretical developments in learning psychology and philosophy in much the same way that many new medical, agricultural, or engineering practices are derived from theoretical advances in the sciences. Without belaboring the issues, we try to illustrate the symbiosis that exists between theory development and advances in educational strategies. We will show this relationship in the course of illustrating strategies for helping students understand how knowledge is constructed by human beings – by students, teachers, and scholars.

To some of our readers, it may come as a surprise to learn that knowledge is *constructed*. That people *discover* knowledge is a common myth. Discovery may play a role in the production of new knowledge, but it is never more than just one of the activities involved in creating new knowledge. The construction of new knowledge begins with our observations of events or objects through the concepts we already possess. By *event* we mean anything that happens or can be made to happen: Lightning is a natural event; wars, schooling, and atom splitting are events people make happen. By *object* we mean anything that exists and can be observed: Dogs, stars, and humans are naturally occurring objects; houses, pottery, and totem poles are objects humans construct. So we see that the construction of knowledge can involve both naturally occurring events or objects and events or objects that humans construct. Knowledge is not discovered like gold or oil, but rather is constructed like cars or pyramids. Let us turn now to the role that concepts play in knowledge making.

We define *concept* as a regularity in events or objects designated by some label. "Chair" is the label we use (in English) to designate an object with legs, a seat, and a back that is used for sitting on. "Wind" is the label we use for the event that involves air in motion. Although it is possible that other animals also recognize regularities in events or objects, humans seem to be unique in their capacity to invent and use language (or symbols) to label and communicate these perceived regularities.[1] Culture is the vehicle through which children acquire concepts that have been constructed over centuries; schools are relatively recent inventions for (we hope) accelerating this process. William James once suggested that the world of the newborn infant is a blooming, buzzing confusion. We don't know if this is true, but we do know that very young infants learn to distinguish the sounds of mother or father coming to feed them and of other important events from the noises around them, and that their cries can signal recognition of these perceived regularities in events. This innate capacity to sort out regularities and to recognize and/or apply labels enables the infant to acquire speech (which all normal children do by age three), an incredible feat that is in many respects the most difficult learning task the individual will ever face. For until children have

---

1. There is some debate as to whether or not chimpanzees and perhaps other higher animals have this capacity, but there can be no debate that humans conceive and use concept labels uniquely well.

constructed this first set of concepts from experience, they cannot use language to recognize and label regularities like those we call trees, kangaroos, winter, or birthday parties. So eager are normal young children to learn new labels, and the regularities they specify, that their repeated questioning can become annoying to parents or older siblings. Children then begin to acquire language rules that, when combined with concept labels, give more precise meaning to events or objects: the request "Milk!" becomes "Me milk!" and later "Please give me some milk to drink." By the time children begin school they have acquired a network of concepts and language rules that play crucial roles in subsequent school learning. Children also learn methods for organizing events or objects that enable them to see new regularities and in turn to recognize the labels that represent those regularities. And this process continues until senescence or death.

We are interested in both learning and knowing. They are not the same. Learning is personal and idiosyncratic; knowing is public and shared. We are interested in thinking, feeling, and acting – all three are present in any educative experience and change the meaning of the experience. Though infant and school child, expert and novice, apprentice and master may share the same experience, the meaning of that experience can be radically different. Educating is the process by which we actively seek to change the meaning of experience. Educating can be liberating or oppressive; this book is committed to making educating more liberating.

THE KNOWLEDGE VEE

In 1977, Gowin invented a heuristic device that we have found to be increasingly useful in helping people understand the structure of knowledge and process of knowledge construction (see Gowin 1981). Figure 1.2 shows a simplified version of Gowin's Vee.

At the point of the Vee are events or objects, and this in one respect is where knowledge production begins; it is a good "point" at which to begin. If we are to observe regularities, we may find it necessary to select specific events or objects in our environment, observe them carefully, and perhaps make some kind of record of our observations. This selection and record-making process will require concepts we already know; the concepts we possess will influence what events or objects we choose to observe and what records we choose to make. These three elements – concepts, events/objects, and records of events/objects (which we call facts) – come together and are intimately intertwined as we try to make new knowledge. When students become muddled about new concepts they are trying to learn, the problem is usually right here at the point of the Vee. The students need to be helped to recognize (1) what events or objects they are observing, (2) what concepts they already know that relate to these events or objects, and (3) what records are worth making.

THE FOUR COMMONPLACES OF EDUCATING

An educational experience is a complex event. It involves four distinct commonplaces, which Schwab (1973) described as teacher, learner, curriculum, and milieu. None of these is reducible to any other, and each must be considered in educating. It is the *teacher's* obligation to set the agenda and to decide what knowledge might be considered and in what sequence. The skilled teacher will of course involve the learner in some aspects of the agenda planning (as in Mastery Learning; see Bloom 1968, 1976), but we expect the teacher to have greater competence than the learner in the area of study. The *learner* must choose to learn; learning is a responsibility that cannot be shared. The *curriculum* comprises the knowledge, skills, and values of the educative experience that meet criteria of excellence that make them worthy of study. The expert teacher will be well versed in both the material and the criteria of excellence used in the area of study. The *milieu* is the context in which the learning experience takes place, and it influences how teacher and student come to share the meaning of the curriculum. Gowin (1981) uses the term *governance* instead of milieu to describe those factors that control the meaning of the educative experience. Schools, thirty-student classes, and state-mandated textbooks are examples of governance factors. In many respects, society, teachers, and curriculum control or govern the meaning of experience, but students also play a role – albeit sometimes a perverse one – by devising what Holt (1964) described as students' "strategies for failure."

We will show how concept mapping and Vee diagramming can have a positive influence on teaching, learning, curriculum, and governance. We will also refer to thinking, feeling, and acting, which, along with the four commonplaces, are part of any significant educational experience. Bear in mind that all seven of these factors are operative in every educational event.

LEARNING AND INSTRUCTION

The philosophical basis of our work makes concepts, and propositions composed of concepts, the central elements in the structure of knowledge and the construction of meaning. The best learning theory that focuses on concept and propositional learning as the basis on which individuals construct their own idiosyncratic meanings is the one proposed by David Ausubel (1963, 1968; Ausubel, Novak, and Hanesian 1978). We will introduce the six key elements of Ausubel's theory as they become relevant to our discussion of the methods we are proposing for improving education and educational research. The primary concept in Ausubel's theory is *meaningful learning,* as contrasted with rote learning. To learn meaningfully, individuals must choose to relate new knowledge to relevant concepts and propositions they already know. In rote learning, on the other hand, new knowledge may be acquired simply by verbatim memorization and arbitrarily incorporated into a person's knowledge structure without interacting with what is already there.

It is important to distinguish between the type of instructional strategy we employ and the kind of learning process in which the student is engaged. Figure 1.3 illustrates that under any instructional strategy, learning can vary from being almost rote to being highly meaningful – from *reception learning,* where information is provided directly to the learner, to autonomous *discovery learning,* where the learner identifies and selects the information to be learned. Much of the educational reform movement of the late 1950s and 1960s was an attempt to get away from rote learning in schools by advancing instructional programs that encouraged discovery, or inquiry learning. Well intentioned as these efforts may have been, they did little to increase the meaningfulness of school learning. The strategies presented in this book are designed to support instructional approaches aimed at increasing meaningful learning.

METAKNOWLEDGE AND METALEARNING

Metaknowledge refers to knowledge that deals with the very nature of knowledge and knowing. Concern with metaknowledge dates to

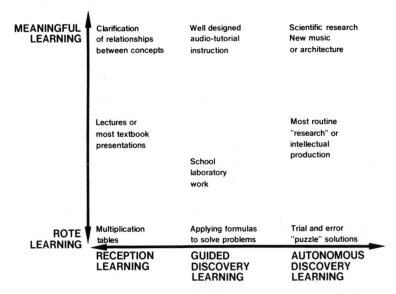

Figure 1.3 Reception learning and discovery learning are on a continuum distinct from that of rote learning and meaningful learning. Typical forms of learning are shown to illustrate where different representative activities would fit into the matrix (see also Figure 8.8).

antiquity, especially to some of the analyses of Socrates, Plato, and Aristotle. The recent rapid advances in knowledge production in the sciences have led to an interest in "metascience," or the study of how sciences work to produce new knowledge, and this interest has in turn stimulated a renewed interest in and concern with metaknowledge.

We see concept mapping and the Vee heuristic as two useful tools for helping students learn about the structure of knowledge and the process of knowledge production, or metaknowledge. Concept mapping has been used successfully with first-grade children and Vee diagramming with upper elementary school students. We believe teachers should make an explicit effort to help students understand knowledge structure and production.

Metalearning refers to learning that deals with the nature of learning, or learning about learning. Hermann Ebbinghaus (1913) was the first psychologist to devote great energy to this, but he was interested in memory, which led him to study the learning of nonsense syllables, or what meaningless information the mind could remember. Systematic study of the learning of meaningful materials is a more recent phenomenon, with the great impetus for such work arising in the 1970s. Our experience with metalearning began when the graduate students who were working with us recognized that the concepts and methods we were using in our research were helping them to "learn how to learn." It occurred to us that it would make sense to teach similar concepts and methods to younger students explicitly to help them learn how to learn. Our early work at Cornell University (Cardemone 1975, Bogden 1977, Moreira 1977) was with college students. More recent work has been with elementary (Kinigstein 1981, Symington and Novak 1982) and secondary students (Gurley 1982, Novak, Gowin, and Johansen 1983).

This book presents our current thinking on and methodologies for educating about metaknowledge and metalearning. We anticipate much activity in this area at Cornell University and elsewhere, and expect to see new ideas and new perceptions promulgated in the future. We caution that so-called memory tricks and other "superlearning" strategies have little or nothing to do with meaningful learning; such promulgations are usually characterized by their avoidance of any discussion of the conceptual nature of knowledge and the processes by which humans construct knowledge. The best metalearning strategies should be accompanied by strategies to aid in metaknowledge learning. Metalearning and metaknowledge are two different but interconnected bodies of knowledge that characterize human understanding. Learning about the nature and structure of knowledge helps students to understand how they learn, and knowledge about learning helps to show them how humans construct new knowledge.

HONESTY AND RESPONSIBILITY IN EDUCATING

We have found that the metalearning and metaknowledge strategies presented in this book have had an unanticipated positive dividend – they promote intellectual honesty on the part of both teachers and students, and this leads to a new sense of responsibility.

Vee diagramming helps us help students to see that in learning, authority resides in the events and objects observed, the validity of the records we choose to make, and the quality or adequacy of the ideas guiding the inquiry. Nobody has absolute authority for making knowledge claims, for no person has *the* right concepts and *the* best way of making records. But lest students think that nothing, therefore, is worth learning, Vee diagramming helps them to see that they can play an active role in judging the validity of claims and that learning becomes meaningful when they take responsibility for doing so.

It is a common belief that learning is automatic and without effort, and that it is continuous and cumulative over life. Yet we have reason, and some evidence, to doubt this belief. Learning has been confused with development, and the biological metaphor of autonomous developmental growth is so powerful that it permeates our thinking. Just consider the tremendous variability in human beings. Most people have a word vocabulary of ten to thirty thousand words, yet Shakespeare is responsible for inventing and writing over three thousand separate puns and had a vocabulary ten times greater than that of most people. Some sailors can tie four or five knots, others more than fifty. Weavers and textile artists of all kinds have a vocabulary of concepts, feelings, and facts about cloth and its colors that vastly surpasses the range of labels comprehensible to most of us. Every human activity, when carried to a point of sufficient proficiency, creates its own concepts, labels, words, actions, and ways of working and wondering that simply exclude the rest of us who are untutored in the events, objects, concepts, and facts about that activity.

We need to cherish, celebrate, and comprehend how beautifully various and inventive human beings are. We need to give up the mythology of continuous development according to simple laws of learning. The possibility for growth and variation is so much greater than the central tendency; the data that seem to justify conventional beliefs about learning are data of aggregation, not facts. Shifting our views on individuality and on how we become individuals will have radical and sweeping consequences.

Why do we feel so strongly about this? First, we have records of the ways of thinking and feeling of hundreds of individuals, and no one is exactly like any other. Second, we have created ways to reveal to people new ways of thinking and feeling that are a great surprise to them. Most human beings don't know what they know. Third, we can present an idea to a person in such a way that it truly changes the meaning of experience for that person; without the idea, living would be very different. First-grade children who learn, meaningfully, the idea of the conservation of matter literally see the world differently, year upon year, than other children sitting next to them ·in the same schoolroom on the same earth. In other words, an education that intervenes in the lives of children creates a world they could never see without the education. True educating changes the meaning of human experience. Fourth, we know that individual persons can learn about learning, can become consciously aware of their power to take charge of their own experience in ways that transform their lives.

One of our stud[ents] sa[id] [he] c[ou]l[d] see imm[edia]tely our new way of looking at edu[cation]. [It] felt it [would] take [him] a year to incorporate all the idea[s] [we] [have] of [think]ing about [it] and teaching mathematics. Yet h[e] [captured] [the] im[portant] con[n]ection between what he had been d[oing]. [He] [has] well [written].

> Unlike the natu[ral] [sciences], [claiming] [objective] validity, [in] mathematics is not t[he] [case] of [a] [single] [truth] [of] [the] teacher.
>
> Any piece of [mathematics] [is] [both] [meaningful] *useful* and *consistent*. [It] [belongs] [to] [the] [system] [that] [expands] [the] universe of our [experience] [and] [is] [to] [be] [able] [to] [use] [th]em, and it should have [internal] consistency and consistency with the larger mathematical sy[stem] [to] [which] it forms [part]. [Whether] these criteria are satisfied is a matter of a[greement] [between] [one] mathematician and another, and between teache[r] and [student]. [The] criteria can be implicitly accepted as binding by tea[chers] [and] students alike. For example, a student can point out a mistake made by a teacher on a blackboard and the teacher has no alternative but to correct it. The teacher is subject to the same rules as the students, and these are not the rules of an authoritarian hierarchy but of a shared structure of concepts – of shared meanings (John Volmink, personal communication).

Such comments highlight what we have come to recognize as the ethics of teaching and learning: showing respect for individual persons and the clarity of their reasoning, and for public and demanding criteria of excellence, such as consistency. When such an ethic is recognized, teaching and learning become something greater than what takes place between two particular persons – teacher and learner – something that both and each of them can appeal to and find appealing. Honesty and responsibility, rather than fakery or fraud, become daily virtues, habitual ways of working that are, indeed, their own reward.

[Handwritten annotation: Of-Trine-Of / This is Roland. Mark hycett book that etc. Got far to buy it / useful for dissertations would be useful for us! R]

CLASSROOM TESTING OF THEORY AND TEACHING TECHNOLOGY

A complicated set of interrelated events occurs in the classroom. For this reason, most psychologists prefer to do research in the laboratory, where variation in events can be rigidly prescribed or controlled. This approach clearly increases the chances for observing regularities in events and hence for creating new concepts. There is, however, a kind of intellectual poverty in this type of research in that the major sources of new experiments (new events) are the concepts and theories that have already been accepted, so that the whole inquiry tends toward circularity. Moreover, such inquiries are controlled more by the available methodologies than by the significance of the research questions themselves. By contrast, the events in classrooms are influenced by students, instructional materials, teachers, the school and community social climate, and a host of interactions among them that vary over time. There is tremendous richness in the extent and variety of teaching and learning events in classrooms, which makes it difficult to observe consistent regularities and hence to form concepts and theories about teaching and learning. It is easy to understand why psychologists stay away from the classroom as a research setting.

For the past fifteen years, most of the research done by our group at Cornell University has focused on classroom observations that test key ideas in Ausubel's learning theory. Partly as a result of our research, Ausubel introduced some modifications into his theory (as reflected in the second edition of *Educational Psychology: A Cognitive View* [1978]). For the past five years, our work has turned increasingly toward developing theory to help design better teaching and learning activities. Concept mapping, as we will describe it, is derived from this work. All viable theories change over time and may eventually be discarded, but we believe Ausubel's cognitive learning theory provides a sound intellectual foundation for creating new teaching and learning events in classrooms that can lead us to improved educational practices over the next few decades.

In all research work, the question arises as to the extent of generalizability of the research findings (or what we will call the *knowledge claims*). Whereas laboratory learning studies have advantages in terms of control over variables in constructed events, it is usually very difficult to generalize from laboratory findings to recommendations for classroom instruction. Educational research workers conducting studies in classrooms have traded some of the control and replicability of laboratory research events for the greater ease of generalizability that comes with research in classroom settings. We attribute the relative fruitlessness of most educational research over the past six or eight decades primarily to the atheoretical nature of most of these studies and their inevitable uselessness for observing regularities that could lead to the construction of viable education concepts. (Our views on educational theory are presented in other books; see Novak 1977a and Gowin 1981.)

Although this book has been written primarily for students, teachers, and parents seeking to obtain a better grasp of the educative process, it is also directed to education research workers. Concept mapping and the other strategies we present not only show promise for improved education practices but they are also, as we will show explicitly in chapter 8, valuable tools for the improvement of educational research.

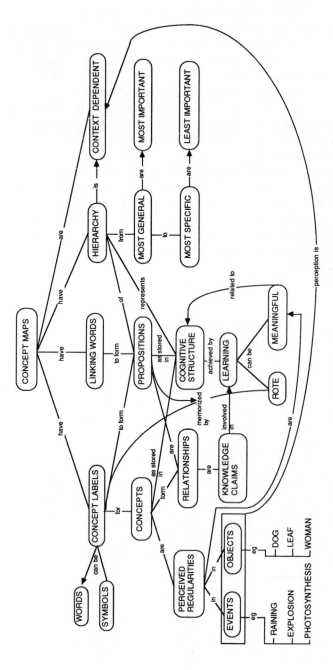

Figure II.o A concept map showing the key features and ideas that underlie concept maps.

2

CONCEPT MAPPING FOR MEANINGFUL LEARNING

CONCEPT MAPS are intended to represent meaningful relationships between concepts in the form of propositions. *Propositions* are two or more concept labels linked by words in a semantic unit. In its simplest form, a concept map would be just two concepts connected by a linking word to form a proposition. For example, "sky is blue" would represent a simple concept map forming a valid proposition about the concepts "sky" and "blue."

Except for a relatively small number of concepts acquired very early by children through a discovery learning process, most concept meanings are learned through the composite of propositions in which the concept to be acquired is embedded. Although concrete empirical props may facilitate concept learning, the *regularity* represented by the concept label is given additional meaning through propositional statements that include the concept. Thus, "grass is green," "grass is a plant," "grass grows," "grass is a monocot," and so on lead to increasing meaning and precision of meaning for the concept "grass." A concept map is a schematic device for representing a set of concept meanings embedded in a framework of propositions.

Concept maps work to make clear to both students and teachers the small number of key ideas they must focus on for any specific learning task. A map can also provide a kind of visual road map showing some of the pathways we may take to connect meanings of concepts in propositions. After a learning task has been completed, concept maps provide a schematic summary of what has been learned.

Because meaningful learning proceeds most easily when new concepts or concept meanings are subsumed under broader, more inclusive concepts, concept maps should be hierarchical; that is, the more general, more inclusive concepts should be at the top of the map, with progressively more specific, less inclusive concepts arranged below

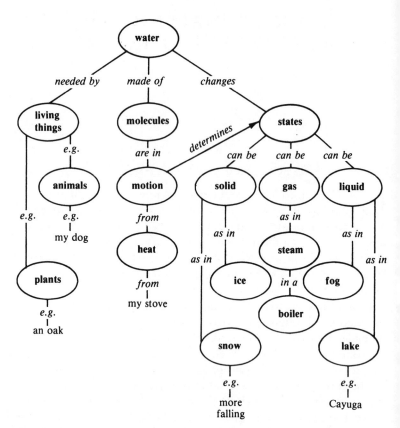

Figure 2.1 A concept map for water showing some related concepts and propositions. Some specific examples of events and objects have been included (in Roman type outside ovals).

them. Figure 2.1 shows such a concept map for water and closely related concepts and Appendix 1 shows a variety of concept maps from several disciplines. As Figure 2.1 shows, it is sometimes helpful to include at the base of the concept map specific objects or events to illustrate the origins of the concept meaning (the regularity being represented).

For different learning segments, the superordinate–subordinate relationships of concepts will change, and we therefore sometimes use the analogy of a rubber sheet for a concept map in which almost any concept on the map can be "lifted up" to the superordinate position, but still retain a meaningful propositional relationship with other concepts on the map. Figure 2.2 shows examples of two "rubber map" configurations.

At first glance it may appear disturbing to see that the same set of concepts can be represented in two or more valid hierarchies. Although we do not understand the specific mechanisms operating in the brain that allow us to store information, it is clear that the neural networks that become established are complex, with many cross connections between functioning brain cells. These networks may account in part for the alternative patterns of meanings available to us when we employ stored concepts to perceive meanings. A somewhat similar phenomenon may be occurring as we shift our visual attention to perceive either a pair of faces or a goblet in the familiar illustration shown in Figure 2.3. Until further advances take place in our understanding of the neurobiology of memory processes, we are limited to models that merely describe the psychological processes that operate in learning and recall of meaningful materials.

Concept mapping is a technique for externalizing concepts and propositions. How accurately concept maps represent either the concepts we possess or the range of relationships between concepts we know (and can express as propositions) can only be conjecture at this time. Undoubtedly, we may develop new concept relationships in the process of drawing concept maps, especially if we seek actively to construct propositional relationships between concepts that were not previously recognized as related: Students and teachers constructing concept maps often remark that they recognize new relationships and hence new meanings (or at least meanings they did not consciously hold before making the map). In this sense, concept mapping can be a creative activity and may help to foster creativity.

The aspect of learning that is distinctly human is our remarkable capacity for using written or spoken symbols to represent perceived regularities in events or objects around us. Language is so much a part of our daily lives that we tend to take it for granted and not to stop and think about how useful language is for translating commonly recognized regularities into code words we can use to describe our thoughts, feelings, and actions. An awareness of the explicit role language plays in the exchange of information is central to understanding the value and purpose of concept mapping and, indeed, central to educating. Educative value is experienced when we recognize that we have grasped a new meaning and feel the emotion

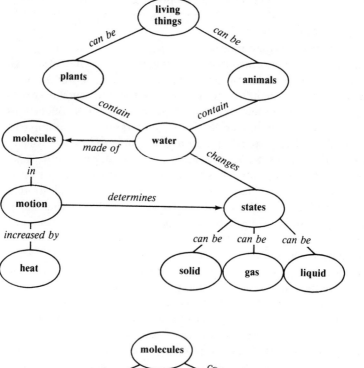

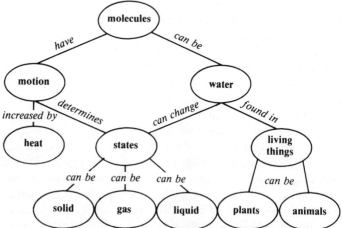

Figure 2.2 Two "rubber map" configurations showing eleven of the concepts in Figure 2.1 in new hierarchical arrangements.

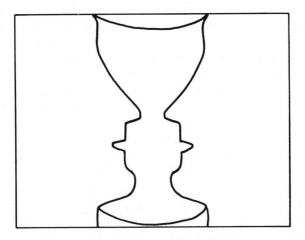

Figure 2.3 Perceptual shift illustrated by reversing figures.

that accompanies this realization. This educative regularity, called *felt significance,* is experienced by the learner to a greater or lesser extent depending on the profundity of the new concept or propositional relationships grasped and their impact on his or her perceptions of related concept meanings. Usually the feelings are positive, but occasionally they may be negative feelings or feelings of fear if we recognize how wrong some of our previous conceptions may have been or how truly ignorant we are about some topic or subject. This fear is a human capacity that we must recognize and encourage as an expression of felt significance.

Ideas that are novel, powerful, and profound are very difficult for us to think about; we need time and some mediating activity to help us. Reflective thinking is controlled doing, involving a pushing and pulling of concepts, putting them together and separating them again. Students need practice in reflective thinking just as teams need time to practice a sport. The making and remaking of concept maps and sharing them with others can be seen as a team effort in the sport of thinking. The computer programs we are now developing may facilitate such practice in thinking with concept maps.

Because concept maps are an explicit, overt representation of the concepts and propositions a person holds, they allow teachers and learners to exchange views on why a particular propositional linkage is good or valid, or to recognize missing linkages between concepts that suggest a need for new learning. Because they contain external-ized expressions of propositions, we have frequently found that con-cept maps are remarkably effective tools for showing misconcep-tions.[1] Misconceptions are usually signaled either by a linkage between two concepts that leads to a clearly false proposition or by a linkage that misses the key idea relating two or more concepts. Figure 2.4 shows examples of missing or faulty conceptions identified in an interview dealing with phases of the moon.

We have found it helpful to think about concept maps as tools for negotiating meanings. What do we mean by negotiating meanings? Let us pause to look at the definition of *negotiate:*

> to confer with another so as to arrive at the settlement of some matter
> ... to deal with (some matter or affair that requires ability for its
> successful handling): MANAGE ... to arrange for or bring about
> through conference, discussion, and compromise (a treaty).[2]

At first glance one may say that if the teacher (or textbook) is supposed to know what is right, how can we suggest that there should be negotiation with the learner? But our answer is that we are speak-ing about cognitive meanings, which cannot be transferred into stu-dents as blood is pumped into veins. Learning the meaning of a piece of knowledge requires dialog, exchange, sharing, and sometimes compromise.

Note that we do not speak about sharing learning. Learning is an activity that cannot be shared; it is rather a matter of individual responsibility. Meanings, on the other hand, can be shared, dis-cussed, negotiated, and agreed upon. When concept mapping is done in groups of two or three students, it can serve a useful social func-tion and also lead to lively classroom discussion. Figure 2.5 shows one of the first concept maps prepared in a junior high school science class. A group of three children shared their ideas on the meaning of a specific textbook passage and jointly constructed this map. Fre-

1   Misconception is the term commonly used to describe an unaccepted (and not necessarily "wrong") interpretation of a concept illustrated in the statement in which the concept is embedded. The expressed meaning is not, however, a mis-conception to the person who holds it, but a functional meaning. Partly for this reason, misconceptions are remarkably stable and may persist for years (see Novak in press). Research suggests that the best method for correcting a misconception is to identify one or more missing concepts that, when integrated into the individ-ual's conceptual framework, will obliterate the misconception.
2   *Webster's Ninth New Collegiate Dictionary* (1983).

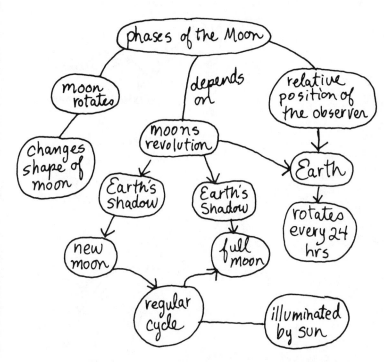

Figure 2.4 A concept map drawn from an interview, showing that this student held the faulty conceptions that the moon's rotation changes the shape (phases) of the moon and that the earth's shadows produce those phases – concepts dealing with the relative positions of the earth and the moon with respect to the sun were missing from the student's conceptual framework.

quently students will (properly) detect ambiguities or inconsistencies in text material and it is helpful for the teacher to step in and clarify concepts or propositions not well presented in the text. It is supportive for students to learn that they are not dull or stupid, but rather that the texts can fail to provide the knowledge needed for shared meaning.

The most important point to remember about sharing meanings in the context of educating is that students always bring something of their own to the negotiation; they are not a blank tablet to be written on or an empty container to be filled. In a manner analogous to the way a professional negotiator may help to bring labor and

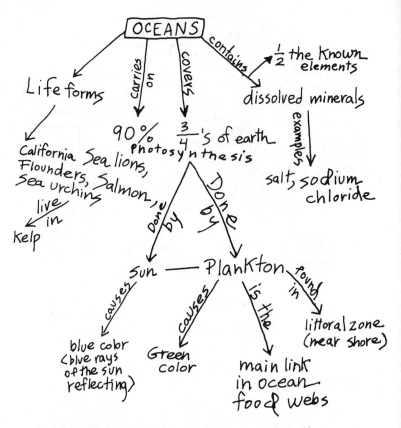

Figure 2.5 A concept map prepared from a science textbook by three seventh-grade students working together.

management together on a contract, concept maps are useful to help students negotiate meanings with their mentors. We will explore this idea further at other points in the book (as we seek to negotiate meanings with the reader). Whatever students have learned before needs to be used to fuel new learning. Both teachers and students need to recognize the value of prior knowledge to acquiring new knowledge.

Referring back to our discussion in Chapter 1 of Schwab's (1973) four commonplaces, we now see that concept maps can play a role in teaching, learning, curriculum, and governance. For the learner, they help to make evident the key concepts or propositions to be learned, and also suggest linkages between the new knowledge and what he or she already knows. For the teacher, concept maps can be used to determine pathways for organizing meanings and for negotiating meanings with students, as well as to point out students' misconceptions. In curriculum planning and organization, concept maps are useful for separating significant from trivial information and for choosing examples. With respect to governance, concept maps help students understand their role as learners; they also clarify the teacher's role and create a learning atmosphere of mutual respect. Concept maps can foster cooperation between student and teacher (or child and school) in a battle in which the "monster" to be conquered is meaninglessness of information and victory is shared meaning.

Once students learn how to prepare concept maps, their maps can be used as powerful evaluation tools. In his *Taxonomy of Educational Objectives* (1956), Bloom outlined six "levels" of objectives in education.[3] It is easy to write objective questions that test whether or not what Bloom called Level I objectives – rote recall of specific information – have been met. But it is exceedingly difficult to design a test to determine whether new knowledge has been analyzed, synthesized, and evaluated by students (Bloom's Level IV–VI objectives). Concept mapping, because it requires students to perform on all six "levels" in one composite effort, makes such evaluation possible. As we will assert in Chapter 5, concept maps' most significant contribution to the improvement of educating may be the ultimate improvement of evaluation techniques, especially as they are applied in research.

Research in most fields is limited by the measurement tools available. We believe one reason educational research has made relatively little progress in the past eighty years has been the serious limitations of our measurement tools (which are mostly objective paper-and-pencil tests). Although Piaget's clinical interview has been proven useful in some settings, it has serious limitations as an evaluation device for large groups and the variety of learning objectives to be

---

3 The validity of the six levels of Bloom's taxonomy has been widely and justifiably criticized. We refer to this work only because it is widely cited in educational literature and because it is well recognized that evaluation of "higher" objectives is at best difficult.

assessed. Concept maps and Vee diagrams can be used to design better interviews, as we will show in Chapter 7, and to improve evaluation in research studies, as we will discuss in Chapter 8.

Our work has also shown concept maps to be useful in curriculum planning and in the design of instruction and educational research, and later chapters will be devoted to discussing their roles in these contexts.

HOW TO INTRODUCE STUDENTS TO CONCEPT MAPPING

As with any act of teaching, there is no one best way to introduce concept mapping. We will present several approaches, all of which have been tried, in one setting or another, and all of which show promise.

In every case, we began by introducing students to the idea of a concept. This introduction can be in the form of a set of activities dealing with learning and memory that we have developed and used with students from junior high school through college, or the idea can be introduced more simply by directly defining concepts, objects, events, and regularities. Table 2.1 shows some of the ways we have found successful for introducing concept mapping to children in grades one to three; Table 2.2 shows strategies that are successful from grades three to seven; and Table 2.3 shows those successful with students from grade seven through college. Although readers will want to examine the table(s) carefully for the age level with which they are most concerned, we will focus our attention on common threads that run through each of these sets of activities.

First, we are advancing the idea that the best way to help students learn meaningfully is to help them explicitly to see the nature and role of concepts and the relationship between concepts as they exist in their minds and as they exist "out there" in the world or in printed or spoken instruction. This is a simple but profound idea; it may take months or years for students to recognize that what they hear, see, touch, or smell is in part dependent on the concepts they have in their minds. This aim is basic to a program to help students learn how to learn.

Second, we are advocating procedures that will help students to extract specific concepts (words) from printed or oral material and

Table 2.1. *Strategies for introducing concept mapping
in grades one to three*

A. *Activities to prepare for concept mapping*

1. Have children close their eyes and ask them if they see a picture in their mind when you recite familiar words, e.g., dog, chair, and grass. Use "object" words at first.

2. Print each word on the board after the children respond. Ask children for more examples.

3. Now continue with "event" words such as raining, skipping, and sewing, and ask children for more examples, writing words on the board.

4. Give the children a few words that are unfamiliar and ask them if they see a picture in their mind. (Scan through a dictionary and find short words that are likely to be unfamiliar to all children, such as "concept.")

5. Help the children recognize that words convey meaning to them when they represent pictures or meanings in their minds.

6. If you have bilingual students in your class, you might introduce a few familiar foreign words to illustrate that different peoples use different labels for the same meaning.

7. Introduce the word *concept* and explain that concept is the word we use to mean some kind of object or event "picture." Review some of the words on the board and ask if these are all concepts; ask if these all bring a picture to mind.

8. Write words on the board such as the, is, are, when, that, then. Ask if these words bring a picture to mind. Children should recognize that those are not *concept* words; they are *linking* words we use in language to link concept words together into sentences that have special meaning.

9. Label your examples "linking words" and ask students for additional examples.

10. Construct short sentences with two concepts and a linking word, e.g., sky is blue, chairs are hard, pencils have lead.

11. Explain to children that most of the words in the dictionary are concept words. (You might have them circle concept words duplicated from a child's dictionary.) Written and spoken language (except that of very young children) uses concept words and linking words.

12. Point out that some words are proper nouns. Names of specific people, places, or things are not concepts.

13. Have children construct some short sentences of their own using

the concept and linking words on the board and some of their own words if they wish.

14. Have one child read a sentence and ask other children which are the concept words and the linking word(s).
15. Introduce the children to the idea that reading is learning how to recognize printed labels for concepts and linking words. Ask if it is easier to read words for which they have a concept in their mind. Point to examples presented earlier of the familiar and unfamiliar concepts and to words such as when, then, while, and there and ask which are usually easiest to read.

B. *Concept mapping activities*
1. Make a list of 10 to 12 related and familiar concept words, organizing these from more general, more inclusive concepts to less general, more specific concepts: For example, plant, stem, root, leaves, flowers, sunlight, green, petals, red, water, air would be a good set of related concepts.
2. Build a concept map on the board or overhead projector and introduce this as, perhaps, a "game we are going to learn to play with words, called concept mapping." See Appendix I for one example of a concept map made from the eleven concepts listed above.
3. Have the children recite some of the short sentences (propositions) shown on the map.
4. Ask if anyone knows a way to connect other concepts to the map, such as water, soil (or dirt), yellow, smell, carrot, cabbage.
5. See if anyone can suggest a cross link between the concepts added and other concepts on the map.
6. Have children copy the map from the board and add two to three of their own concepts (and cross links if they can).
7. Give children lists of related words and have them construct their own concept maps. Appendix I shows lists of words and sample concept maps constructed by first-grade children. Children were given the option of choosing which list of words they wanted to map.
8. If space permits, have children show their concept maps on the board and ask a few to explain the story their concept map tells. Avoid criticism of concept maps at this point and overemphasize positive attributes to help make concept mapping a positive affective experience. You will probably find that students who · often do poorly in other classwork will make good concept maps

Table 2.1. *(cont.)*

with good cross links (albeit they may misspell words or write illegibly). This would be a good opportunity to encourage these children. If space is limited, concept map papers might be taped up on walls or cabinets for children (and perhaps parents) to observe and share.

9. Take some time to point out positive features of children's concept maps, e.g., especially good hierarchies or interesting cross links.

10. Select a short (10–30 sentence) familiar story or section from reading materials and duplicate copies for all children. Help them to identify some of the concept words in the story and some of the linking words. Select a passage that has some meaning, that is, some message about the world or about people.

11. Ask the children which concepts are most needed to tell what the story is all about, and have them circle the key concepts in their copy of the text.

12. Have children prepare a list of concepts from the story, listing first the concepts that are most important in the story and going down the list to concepts that are less important.

13. Discuss the children's list and then construct with them a concept map for the story. Appendix I shows an example of how this can be done.

14. Have the children construct their own concept map for the story, using activities similar to those for concept maps constructed from word lists.

15. Choose new stories (two or more) and duplicate copies for the children. Have children select stories and replicate activities done as a class: circle key concept words; prepare a list of concept words from most important to least important; and draw a concept map for their story.

16. Have some children read their stories to the class using only their concept map. See if the class can determine what the story is about.

17. Concept maps for each child could be posted about the room, together with the stories, for other people to see.

18. Have the children prepare a concept map for something they know most about (e.g., baseball, violin, swimming, autos) and present it to the class. An overhead projector would be helpful here, with children preparing transparencies before class, or you could have a few children each day draw their maps on the board. As with other maps, emphasize positive attributes and

Table 2.1. *(cont.)*

---

avoid negative criticism (other children usually offer plenty of this).
19. Have children write a short story based on their concept maps. Some of these might be read to the class.
20. From here on, almost any classroom activity should be relatable to concepts and concept maps. You might encourage children to paper the walls of their rooms at home with their own concept maps. Also, help them to see that one concept map can be linked to another and that all of the concepts we have are in at least some remote way linked to each other. This cross linking is what makes us "smart."

---

to identify relationships among those concepts. Here it is necessary to isolate *concepts* and *linking words* and to recognize that although both are important language units, they have different roles in conveying meaning.

A third key idea we want to express is that concept maps present a way to visualize concepts and the hierarchical relationships between them. Whereas most humans have a notoriously poor memory for recall of specific details, their capacity for recall of specific visual images is remarkable – we can easily recognize our close friends in a gathering of hundreds or in a photograph of a group. It would be extraordinarily difficult to program a sophisticated computer to make similarly reliable recognitions. Concept mapping has a potential for enlisting this human capacity for recognizing patterns in images to facilitate learning and recall. Much research is needed on this issue, and we hope this book will stimulate it. It would, of course, be disastrous if teachers expected students to memorize concept maps and be able to reproduce them in content, structure, and detail precisely as they were shown to the class. This would require the most demanding kind of rote recall, the polar opposite of the type of learning activity we are trying to encourage. We do not mean that any kind of concept map is as good as any other. In Table 2.4 we offer specific suggestions for evaluating concept maps, and we will discuss the use of concept maps for evaluation of learning further in Chapter 5.

We also want to emphasize that concept maps become increasingly more useful as students become more proficient at labeling the

Table 2.2. *Strategies for introducing concept mapping in grades three to seven*

A. *Activities to prepare for concept mapping*
   1. Make two lists of words on the blackboard or overhead projector using a list of familiar words for objects and another list for events. For example, object words might be car, dog, chair, tree, cloud, book; and event words could be raining, playing, washing, thinking, thunder, birthday party. Ask children if they can describe how the two lists differ.
   2. Ask the children to describe what they think of when they hear the word car, dog, etc. Help them recognize that even though we use the same words, each of us may think of something a little different. These mental images we have for words are our *concepts;* introduce the word concept.
   3. Repeat the activities in step 2, using event words. Again, point out the differences in our mental images, or concepts, of events. You may want to suggest at this point that one reason we have trouble understanding each other sometimes is that our concepts are never quite identical even though we know the same words. Words are labels for concepts, but each of us must acquire our own meanings for words.
   4. Now list words such as are, where, the, is, then, with. Ask children what comes to their minds when they hear each of these words. These are not concept words; we call them *linking* words and we use them in speaking and writing. Linking words are used together with concept words to construct sentences that have meaning.
   5. Proper nouns are not concept words but rather names of specific people, events, places, or objects. Use some examples and help children to see the distinction between labels for *regularities* in events or objects and those for specific events or objects (or proper nouns).
   6. Using two concept words and linking word(s), construct a few short sentences on the board to illustrate how concept words plus linking words are used by humans to convey meanings. Examples would be: The dog is running. or, There are clouds and thunder.
   7. Have the students construct a few short sentences of their own, identify the concept words and tell whether each is an object or event, and also identify the linking words.
   8. If you have bilingual children in the class, have them present some foreign words that label the same events or objects. Help

29

Table 2.2. *(cont.)*

the children recognize that language does not make the concept but only serves as the label we use for the concept. If we learn words but fail to learn what kind of regularity in objects or events the words represent, we have not learned new concepts.

9. Introduce some short but unfamiliar words to the class such as dire, terse, or *canis*. These are words that stand for concepts they already know, but have somewhat special meaning. Help children see that meanings of concepts are not rigid and fixed, but can grow and change as we learn more.

10. Choose a section of a textbook (one page is sufficient) and duplicate copies for the children. Choose a passage that conveys a definite message. As a class, ask them to read the passage and identify key concepts. (Usually 10 to 20 relevant concepts can be found in a single page of text material.) Also have the children note some linking words and concept words that are less important to the story line.

B. *Concept mapping activities*

1. Have the children rank order the concepts they have found in a text page from most general, most inclusive to least general, least inclusive. Their lists may vary, but they should recognize that some concepts are more salient to the story line than others. Now help them to construct a concept map using the concepts from their lists. This might be done on the blackboard.

2. For homework or seatwork, choose several other text passages and have students construct a map (using steps 9 and 10). There is value in having two or more children map the same text selection and later compare maps. We have also found it helpful to have students work in twos or threes to construct a map; much good discussion among students can occur. Individual or group maps can be put on the board or overhead projector and explained to the class.

3. A good way to help students recognize that good maps capture the essential meanings in a text is to have them read their map as a story one or two days after it was completed. Students who construct good maps will show remarkable fidelity in reproducing the meaning of text, even though they have not memorized the text.

Table 2.2. *(cont.)*

4. Make up two or more lists of concept words from some topic recently discussed in class. The words should be related, that is, they should have relevance to a common theme. Let students choose the topic of the word list and then have them repeat step 1 above.
5. After each student has constructed a few maps, it would be useful to introduce them to scoring procedures given in Table 2.4. Take one of the group-constructed maps and show them how it would be scored. Table 2.4 shows a sample of a map scored according to the criteria. Have students score one of their own concept maps and, showing the map on the board or overhead projector, ask a few students to explain their scoring values.
6. Have a "progress discussion" with the class:
   a. Review with them the definitions of concept, object, events, linking words, proper nouns.
   b. Remind them that some concepts, such as ice skate, volcanic explosion, or high achiever, are labeled by two or more words, even though they comprise simpler, more general concepts.
   c. Discuss the idea that we learn best when we tie new concepts to concepts we already have.
   d. Point out that hierarchically constructed maps help to subsume more specific concept meanings into larger, more general concepts.
   e. Help them to see that cross links on their maps mean they are tying together concepts that might not otherwise be seen as related. This cross tying or integrating of concept meanings favors retention and later use of concepts, especially in problem solving or creating new materials (new stories, poems, music, or experiments).
   f. Discuss alternative weightings for criteria in the scoring key and perhaps construct your own alternative key for scoring concept maps.
7. Discuss students' feelings about concept mapping, rote learning, and meaningful learning.

Learning how to learn

Table 2.3. *Strategies for introducing concept mapping in grades seven through college*

A. *Activities to prepare for concept mapping*
   1. Make two lists of words on the blackboard or overhead projector using a list of familiar words for objects and another list for events. For example, object words might be car, dog, chair, tree, cloud, book; and event words could be raining, playing, washing, thinking, thunder, birthday party. Ask the students if they can describe how the two lists differ. Try to help them recognize that the first list is things or *objects* and the second list is happenings or *events,* and label the two lists.
   2. Ask the students to describe what they think of when they hear the word car, dog, etc. Help them recognize that even though we use the same words, each of us may think of something a little different. These mental images we have for words are our *concepts;* introduce the word concept.
   3. Repeat the activities in step 2, using event words. Again, point out the differences in our mental images, or concepts, of events. You may want to suggest at this point that one reason we have trouble understanding each other sometimes is that our concepts are never quite identical even though we know the same words. Words are labels for concepts, but each of us must acquire our own meanings for words.
   4. Now list words such as are, where, the, is, then, with. Ask students what comes to their minds when they hear each of these words. These are not *concept* words; we call them *linking* words and we use them in speaking and writing. Linking words are used together with concept words to construct sentences that have meaning.
   5. Proper nouns are not concept words but rather names of specific people, events, places, or objects. Use some examples and help students to see the distinction between labels for *regularities* in events or objects and those for specific events or objects (or proper nouns).
   6. Using two concept words and linking word(s), construct a few short sentences on the board to illustrate how concept words plus linking words are used by humans to convey meanings. Examples would be: The dog is running. or, There are clouds and thunder.
   7. Have students construct a few short sentences of their own, identify the concept words and tell whether each is an object or event, and also identify the linking words.

32

Table 2.3. *(cont.)*

8. If you have bilingual students in the class, have them present some foreign words that label the same events or objects. Help the students recognize that language does not make the concept, but only serves as the label we use for the concept.
9. Introduce some short but unfamiliar words to the class such as dire, terse, or *canis*. These are words that stand for concepts they already know, but have somewhat special meaning. Help students see that meanings of concepts are not rigid and fixed, but can grow and change as we learn more.
10. Choose a section of a textbook (one page is sufficient) and duplicate copies for the students. Choose a passage that conveys a definite message. As a class, ask them to read the passage and identify key concepts. (Usually 10 to 20 relevant concepts can be found in a single page of text material.) Also have the students note some linking words and concept words that are less important to the story line.

B. *Concept mapping activities*
   1. Select a particularly meaningful paragraph or two from a text or other printed material. Have the students read the text and select the key concepts, that is, those concepts necessary for understanding the meaning of the text. List these concepts on the board (or overhead projector) as they are identified. Now discuss with the students which concept is the most important, most inclusive idea in the text.
   2. Put the most inclusive concept at the head of a new list of rank-ordered concepts. List the next most general, most inclusive concepts, working through the first list until all concepts are rank ordered. There will not always be agreement among the students on the ordering, but usually only a few major differences in ranking of the concepts will arise. This is OK because it suggests that there may be more than one way to see the meaning of the text.
   3. Now begin constructing a concept map, using the rank-ordered list as a guide in building the concept hierarchy. Have students help in choosing good linking words to form the propositions shown by the lines on the map. One good way to have them practice map making is to have students write concept words and linking words on paper rectangles and then rearrange these rectangles as they get new insights on the map organization. (See Figure 2.10.)

Table 2.3. *(cont.)*

4. Now look for cross links between concepts in one section of the map and concepts in another part of the concept "tree." Have students help to choose linking words for the cross links.

5. Most first effort maps have poor symmetry or some concept clusters poorly located relative to other more closely related concepts or clusters of concepts. Reconstruct the map if this would be helpful. Point out to students that at least one and sometimes two or three reconstructions of a map are needed to show a good representation of propositional meanings as they understand them.

6. Discuss the concept map scoring criteria in Table 2.4 and score the concept map constructed. Point out possible structural changes that might improve the meaning, and perhaps the score, of the map.

7. Have the students select a section of text or other material and repeat steps 1–6 on their own (or in groups of two or three).

8. Student-constructed maps can be presented to the class on the blackboard or overhead projector. "Reading" the map should make clear to other students in the class what the text was about, as interpreted by the map maker.

9. Have students construct a concept map for ideas important in a hobby, sport, or special interest they have. These might be posted around the room and informal discussion encouraged.

10. Incorporate one or two concept mapping questions in your next test to illustrate that concept mapping is a valid evaluation procedure that demands hard thinking and can illustrate understanding of the subject matter.

lines. When we first used concept maps, we seldom labeled lines on the assumption that whoever "read" a map could fill in satisfactory linking words. This proved to be true, however, only for persons thoroughly familiar with the learning activities the specific concept map was concerned with; it soon became apparent that most others, even those who knew much about the subject matter and about school settings similar to ours, could not make sense out of many of our maps. We now consider careful attention to the words selected to link concepts an essential aspect of instruction in concept mapping. This is not to suggest that one and only one correct linking word exists. Often there are two or three equally valid ways to link two concepts, but each will have a slightly different connotation. For example, if we link the concepts *water* and *ice* with words such as *can be, becomes, sometimes is,* each proposition thus generated has a similar but not identical meaning. The changes in meaning become even more conspicuous when other, related concepts are linked to water and/or ice. If we add the concept *molecule* to our map, new relationships and new meanings involving ice, water, and molecules can be shown. Concept maps are thus powerful tools for observing the nuances of meaning a student holds for the concepts embedded in his or her map. When concept maps are conscientiously constructed, they are remarkably revealing of students' cognitive organization.

Sometimes it is useful to apply arrows to linking lines to show that the meaning relationship expressed by the linking word(s) and concepts is primarily in one direction. Ordinarily, hierarchical maps imply relationships between higher level concepts and subordinate ones. To reduce clutter on the map, we use the convention that no arrows are shown unless the relationship indicated is something other than a superordinate to subordinate linkage between two concepts. This convention also helps to accentuate the directionality of those relationships that are linked by arrows. Figure 2.6 shows a sample concept map drawn with arrows indicating some relationships.

Concept maps need to be redrawn. The first concept map a person makes is almost certain to have flaws: It may have been difficult to show important hierarchical relationships between concepts, or some concepts closely linked in meaning with others may be on the wrong side of the map so that the cross-link lines go all over the paper. We find that a second map usually shows key relationships more explicitly. Most students will not have the patience or interest to try a third or fourth version of their map for a topic, but they should be encouraged at least to make a second version.

A secondary important reason for redrawing maps is to clean them up – to make them neater, correct spelling errors, and reduce clutter or crowding. Most students need constant encouragement to improve their penmanship and to express themselves more clearly. Concept mapping can help to provide that encouragement, for redoing a map always involves more than simply making it look neater. The clarity of the relationships between the concepts illustrated on the map can always be improved on the revision, and thus there is an important added incentive for redoing maps – increasing the meaningfulness

Table 2.4. *Scoring criteria for concept maps*

1. *Propositions.*   Is the meaning relationship between two concepts indicated by the connecting line and linking word(s)? Is the relationship valid? For each meaningful, valid proposition shown, score 1 point. (See scoring model below.)
2. *Hierarchy.*   Does the map show hierarchy? Is each subordinate concept more specific and less general than the concept drawn above it (in the context of the material being mapped)? Score 5 points for each valid level of the hierarchy.
3. *Cross links.*   Does the map show meaningful connections between one segment of the concept hierarchy and another segment? Is the relationship shown significant and valid? Score 10 points for each cross link that is both valid and significant and 2 points for each cross link that is valid but does not illustrate a synthesis between sets of related concepts or propositions. Cross links can indicate creative ability and special care should be given to identifying and rewarding its expression. Unique or creative cross links might receive special recognition, or extra points.
4. *Examples:*   Specific events or objects that are valid instances of those designated by the concept label can be scored 1 point each. (These are not circled because they are not concepts.)
5. In addition, a criterion concept map may be constructed, and scored, for the material to be mapped, and the student scores divided by the criterion map score to give a percentage for comparison. (Some students may do better than the criterion and receive more than 100% on this basis).

of the composition – that is absent or less conspicuous in other forms of expository expression. We have found a greater willingness, especially in boys, to redo concept maps than to rewrite reports or themes. It is a good idea to get students used to redrawing their concept maps by asking to see both the first and second versions of the first map they draw, and continuing at least periodically to request multiple versions of their maps.

Concept maps as we have described them are not the only ways to represent meanings. Examples of other representational forms are shown in Figure 2.7. Flow charts are often used to represent sequences

Table 2.4. *(cont.)*

Scoring Model

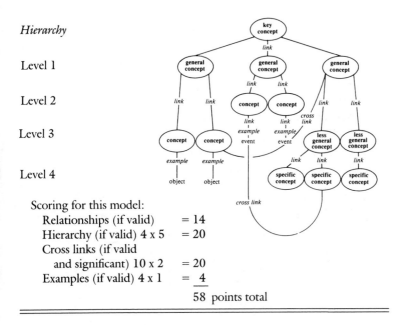

Hierarchy

Level 1

Level 2

Level 3

Level 4

Scoring for this model:
Relationships (if valid)	= 14
Hierarchy (if valid) 4 x 5	= 20
Cross links (if valid and significant) 10 x 2	= 20
Examples (if valid) 4 x 1	= 4
	58 points total

of activities. Organizational charts may show a hierarchy, but they represent administrative units and/or functions, not concept meanings. Cycles, such as the water cycle, are often used in science. Semantic networks and predicability trees are used in some psychological and linguistic writings. But none of these forms of maps are based on the theory of learning and theory of knowledge that underlie concept mapping strategies and their application to education. We believe that concept mapping, as described in this book, has more promise than other relationship schemes for both educating and research.

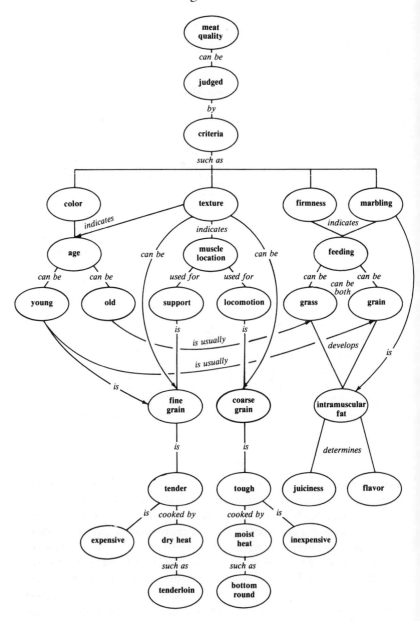

Figure 2.6 Concept map prepared for a course in meat science. Arrows show cross linkages.

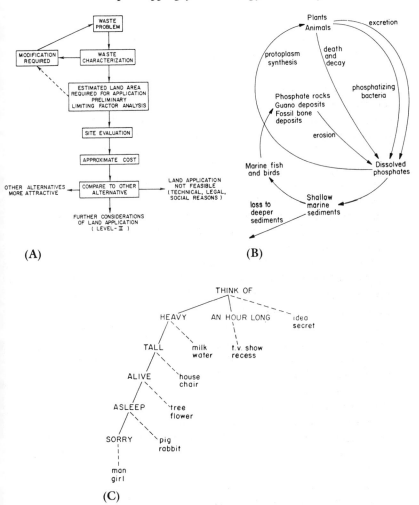

Figure 2.7 Flow charts **(A)**, cycle diagrams **(B)**, and predicability trees **(C)** are three other ways to represent concepts. None of these forms, however, is consistent with Ausubelian learning theory. (Figure 2.7**A** from Loehr et al. 1979, published by Van Nostrand Reinhold, and reprinted by permission from the Wadsworth Publishing Company, Belmont CA. Figure 2.7**B** from Goodnight et al. 1979, published by Van Nostrand Reinhold, and reprinted by permission from the Wadsworth Publishing Company. Figure 2.7**C** from Keil 1979, reprinted by permission from Harvard University Press, Cambridge, Mass.)

EDUCATIONAL APPLICATIONS OF
CONCEPT MAPPING

Exploration of what the learners already know. In Chapter 1 we pointed out that meaningful learning requires a deliberate effort on the part of learners to relate new knowledge to relevant concepts they already possess. To facilitate this process, both teacher and student, if they are to proceed most efficiently in meaningful learning, need to know the "conceptual starting place." In the epigraph to *Educational Psychology: A Cognitive View,* David Ausubel says, "If I had to reduce all of educational psychology to just one principle, I would say this: The most important single factor influencing learning is what the learner already knows. Ascertain this and teach him accordingly" (Ausubel 1968 [2nd ed. 1978]).

Ausubel was not simply restating an old idea, for he devoted five chapters of his book to illustrating how the concepts and propositions the learner knows play a central role in meaningful (as distinct from rote) learning. Despite this lengthy and precise elucidation of the theoretical issues, however, he has not provided educators with simple, functional tools to help them ascertain "what the learner already knows." Concept mapping is such an educational tool; it has been developed specifically to tap into a learner's cognitive structure and to externalize, for both the learner and the teacher to see, what the learner already knows. We do not claim that a concept map is a complete representation of the relevant concepts and propositions the learner knows, but we do claim that it is a workable approximation, from which both students and teachers can consciously and deliberately expand and move forward.

Once students have acquired the basic skill of concept mapping, six or eight *key concepts* can be selected that are central to understanding the topic or area of instruction to be covered, and students are asked first to build a concept map relating those concepts and then to bring in additional relevant concepts and link them to form propositions that have meaning. It may be useful to rank order the concepts first presented if there are significant hierarchical relationships among them. Another approach would be to help students identify three or four major concepts in a section or chapter of their textbook and use these concepts to begin the construction of a concept map. The students can then more easily identify other relevant concepts

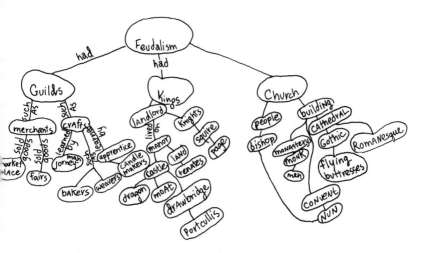

Figure 2.8 A concept map for history prepared by a previously low-achieving student in sixth grade.

and add these to form their own concept maps. Figure 2.8 shows a map prepared by a sixth-grade student from a history text. The map segment showing feudalism, guilds, kings, and church was drawn by the teacher, and the student added the other concepts. Note that not all lines were labeled, a common problem that only constant encouragement can correct. Nevertheless, the map does represent a good hierarchical organization of subordinate with higher order concepts. If the text had presented specific events or objects (e.g., names of kings or manors), students could also have added these in appropriate places. Incidentally, the student who drew the map in Figure 2.8 was usually a C or D student, partly because he consistently refused to do much of the less meaningful work required. His map (and others he drew) was subsequently used as a basis for class discussions, and his grades improved markedly over the remainder of the school year. We have found that many students classified as "learning disabled" are really bright children who lack the skill and/or motivation for rote mode learning, but who can move to the front of the class when they are given an opportunity for creative, meaningful representation of their knowledge (Melby-Robb 1982).

Meaningful use of concept maps as a preinstructional tool is best arrived at by (1) giving careful thought to the choice of key concept labels selected as the base for the map, (2) helping students to keep searching their cognitive structures for relevant concepts, (3) helping students construct propositions between the concepts provided and the concepts they know by helping them to choose good linking words or perhaps to recognize what other, more general concepts fit into the hierarchy, and (4) helping them to discriminate between specific objects or events and the more inclusive concepts those events or objects represent.

The end product of this preinstruction mapping will be a good conceptual benchmark from which students can construct richer meanings. It will also serve the important purpose of illustrating conceptual growth: After three weeks of instruction, the students may be surprised to see how much they have elaborated, refined, and cross related concepts in their own cognitive structures. Nothing has more positive affective impact on encouraging meaningful learning than demonstrated success in substantive accomplishment of meaningful learning. Figure 2.9 shows two concept maps drawn by a basketball player, one early in the season, the other after several months of coaching (see also Figure 2.12). What we should pay attention to is a student's capacity to identify and enrich the meaning of his or her experience. (We are not advocating mere success by the students in achieving and producing maps; recognizing and valuing the change in meaning in human experience is the educational value.)

Roadmapping a learning route. We have already noted that concept maps are somewhat analogous to road maps in that they show relationships, not between places, but between ideas. Concept maps can help learners chart a course to get from where they are to the final objective. If you were planning an auto trip from, say, New York to Seattle via Houston you would probably begin with a national map showing interstate highways and the major cities en route. Next, you might look at individual state maps to locate interesting places to stop for meals, sightseeing, and sleeping. Finally, you might refer to local maps to plan specific routes through a city to a place of interest.

In much the same way, we can construct a global concept map showing the major ideas to be considered in a semester or a year, then move to specific concept maps showing a three- or four-week segment, and, finally, draw a detailed concept map for one or a few days of instruction. Just as with road maps, these three levels of magnification are useful to help learners to acquire and to recall a rich store of detailed impressions, coordinated ideas and meanings, and vivid feelings and images. A glance at the "big map" should facilitate easy recall of various details observed en route.

One advantage we have in the classroom over a passenger in a car is that we can hang our maps – global, more specific, and detailed – on the walls so that both students and teacher can easily see where we are, where we have been, and where we are going. Walls are often enhanced by interesting wallpaper, so why not paper the walls with concept maps? To make the wall maps more interesting (and also of greater educational value) photos or pictures representing key concepts can be pasted on them in order to illustrate specific objects or events encountered, or to be encountered, during the conceptual journey and to "pump" meaning into the framework of more abstract regularities the concept labels represent.

Extracting meaning from textbooks. Learning to read effectively presents a dilemma. Words and phrases are hard to read when they have little or no meaning, yet reading is a powerful way to learn meanings. How do we break the cycle: How do we acquire meaning without first reading a text, and how do we read a text that has little meaning for us? Concept mapping can help to break through the meaning impasse.

A concept map with as few as six or eight concepts and propositions can give a general road map for reading a particular passage and help to break the meaningless – hard-to-read cycle. Figure 2.10 gives a brief example of a concept map for a small segment of text. This map was made by having the student write key concept words on paper rectangles and then move them, together with linking words, until a satisfying concept map was formed. It is obviously impracticable to devise concept maps for every paragraph or page of a textbook. But it is not an overwhelming task to work with students and sketch out together a map of the key ideas in a section or chapter. The 10 or 15 minutes this might take could not only save the students time in subsequent reading, but will also significantly enhance the meanings they will extract from the text. Moreover, because some misconceptions are almost sure to exist for any chapter-size segment of reading, *premapping* can clue students as to what misinterpretations they should watch out for as they read. Sometimes the greatest hindrance to extracting meaning from a text segment is what we think we already know, which may be either not true or significantly

Figure 2.9 Two concept maps prepared by a basketball player, one (above) early in training and the other (facing page) late in the season. Note the increased complexity and integration of concepts, which was accompanied by much-improved player performance.

at variance with the view the text is presenting. We do not want students to believe that the printed text is always right, but we do need to help them to critically assess what the text is saying and what they come to believe after reading it.

Global and specific concept maps constructed for readings can help a student journey through the material for a whole course of instruction in a more meaningful way. The challenge is to help learners see the relevance of the global conceptual road map before they read the

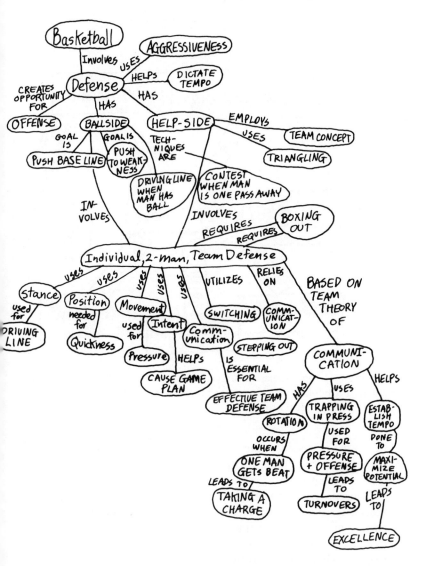

text. Here, again, we are in a kind of "catch 22," where the global concept meanings to be developed in the text are part of what the learner needs in order to read the text meaningfully. We break out of this trap only if we are skillful in devising global concept maps

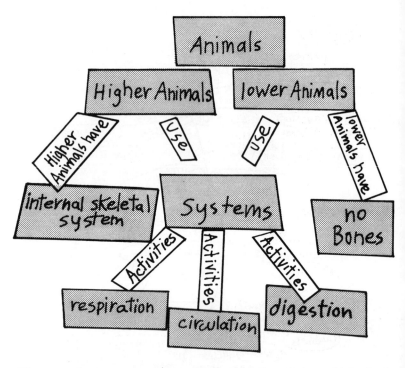

Figure 2.10 A concept map constructed from a section of a junior high school science textbook in which paper rectangles were used to permit easy modification of concept relationships.

that organize the ideas the students already have that can be brought to bear on the readings. This is where teaching becomes an art as well as a science.

Concept maps can be useful not only for understanding typical school textbooks but also for better understanding literary works such as novels. Figure 2.11 is a concept map prepared from *Eveline,* a story by James Joyce. Key ideas in the book are presented in a simple map, which can in turn be used as a basis for lively class discussions. Asking students to prepare concept maps to report on literary readings means that they must not only read a work, but also make some conceptual sense out of it. One of our former students developed a general concept map showing key concepts that can be found in any literary work, and this is included in Appendix I (Figure I.6).

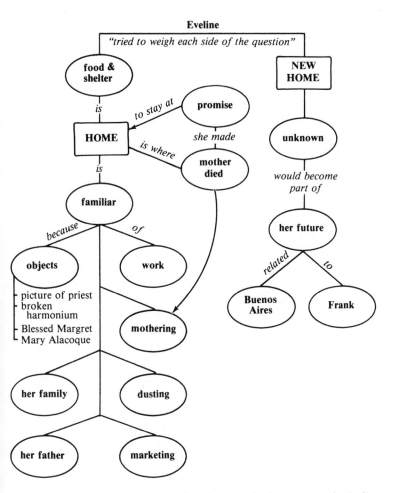

Figure 2.11 A concept map prepared to illustrate the key concepts in *Eveline, a novel* by James Joyce.

Extracting meanings from laboratory, studio, and/or field studies. Often students enter into a laboratory, studio, or field setting wondering what they are supposed to do or see; and their confusion is so great that they may not get as far as asking what regularities in events or objects they are to observe, or what relationships between concepts are significant. As a result, they proceed blindly to make records, manipulate apparatus, or make constructions with little purpose and little consequent enrichment of their understanding of the relationships they are observing or manipulating. Concept maps can be used to help students identify key concepts and relationships, which in turn will help them to interpret the events and objects they are observing.

One could argue that there is value in any observation or manipulation of real-world materials, and to some extent this may be true. The touch, smell, taste, and texture of materials do provide some of the raw perceptions needed to construct perceived regularities (i.e., concepts). Furthermore, some would contend that cognitive or conceptual knowledge has little bearing on many manipulative learning activities. We would agree with Herrigel (1973), who has argued that expertise in something as motor-skill centered as archery requires first a recognition of the conceptual nature, purpose, and feel of the bow and arrow. Achievement in nearly every area of human endeavor would probably be enhanced if the relevant concepts and how they function were understood and used to interpret events or objects. Figure 2.12 is a concept map developed by one of our graduate students to help the basketball players he coached improve their performance. We have found that every skill is an action that can be seen more explicitly when the set of concepts that conveys the meaning of the action is identified and mapped.

Field trips have a recognized potential for being rich educational experiences, but too often they are little more than school social outings. A principal problem is that too often neither leaders nor participants know what they are to observe or what meaning these observations are supposed to convey. Students need to go into the field equipped with a framework of potential meaning, so that they will be able to interpret their observations, and a concept map can be a highly effective way to construct that framework. Figure 2.13 shows a concept map used to plan a field trip to a nature center where fifth- and sixth-grade students were to observe, among other things, the ecology of a rotting log. The map served as the basis both for planning classroom instruction on the topic before the trip and for discussing it with the students afterward. Kinigstein (1981) found that when concept maps were used in this way, students made positive gains in their understanding of ecological concepts as a result of their class and field experiences and were overwhelmingly positive in their attitudes toward the field work. Concept maps not only help students to gain meaningful knowledge from field experiences, they also enhance positive feeling and acting during and after the experience.

Reading articles in newspapers, magazines, and journals. We have found concept mapping to be a good "shorthand" for taking notes on papers or articles in newspapers, magazines, and technical journals. After a quick reading of an article, it is relatively easy to go back and circle key concepts or propositions and then to construct a concept map representing them in a hierarchical order. Constructing a concept map enables one to identify the most important concept(s) and/or propositions and to restate in a concise way the major points made in the article. The hierarchical organization of the concept map casts the meaning of ideas in the article into a framework that makes it easy to recall the substance of the article and to review the information presented in it. Figure 2.14 shows a concept map prepared from a journal article dealing with the value of coaching for improving SAT scores.

In order for a map to show a clearer and more complete set of relationships between the concepts or propositions in an article, key concepts or propositions must often be added to it. One of the reasons we often have trouble reading short journal articles or papers in a field unfamiliar to us is that some of the important concepts and propositions we need to capture the meanings of the main ideas are not repeated, not in the best position in the article, or missing entirely. A person familiar with the field will unconsciously fill in concepts or propositions and not even notice that the article is conceptually incomplete. There are very few writers who can prepare articles for lay readers on technical material; most "experts" tend to leave out explicit descriptions of key concepts or propositions that are very familiar to them, making their writing conceptually opaque to the lay reader. Concept mapping may be especially useful for preparing articles on technical subjects that lay persons can read and understand. We will have more to say on this subject in Chapter 4.

Planning a paper or exposition. Most students find writing a paper almost frightening; they simply cannot get their ideas together when they sit down to write. There is something terribly intimidating about the stare of a blank sheet of paper. Concept mapping is one way to ease over this hurdle. It is fairly easy to list a few concepts or propositions one wants or needs to include in a paper. Next, usually in a

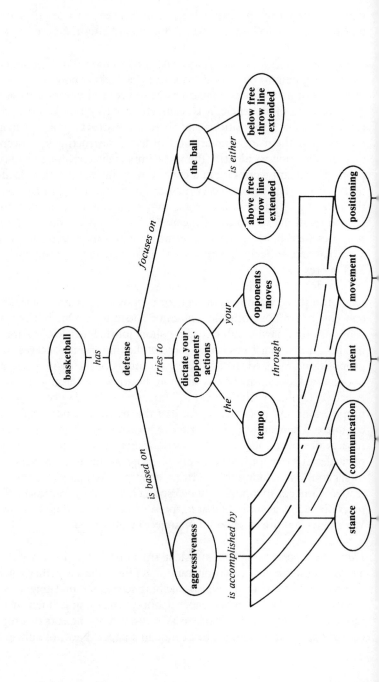

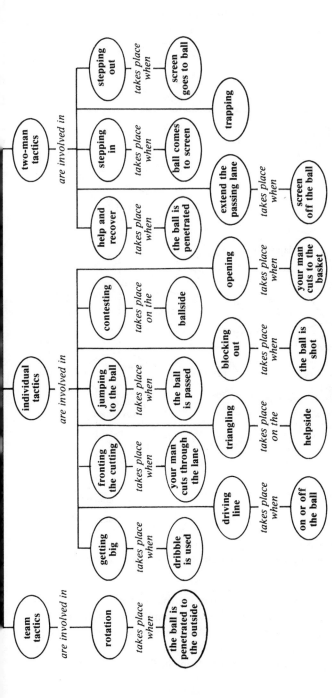

Figure 2.12 A concept map prepared by Brad Nadborne to guide his players in basketball training (see also Figure 2.9).

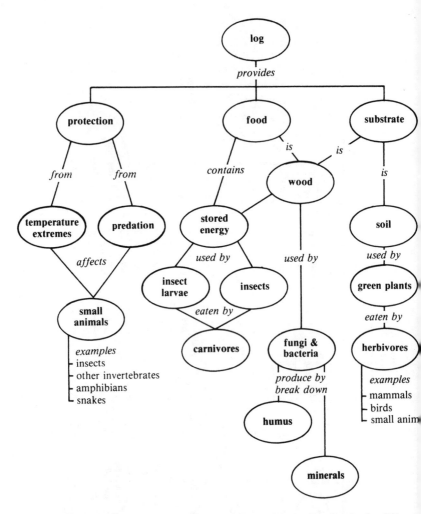

Figure 2.13 A concept map used to prepare an instructional unit, for fifth- and sixth-grade students, on a rotting log observed on a field trip.

few minutes, a brief concept map can be constructed – not a complete map with all the ideas, but one complete enough to guide the writing of that first paragraph. As a matter of course, a good first paragraph for most papers probably is a clear statement of the top four or five concepts and propositions in this concept map.

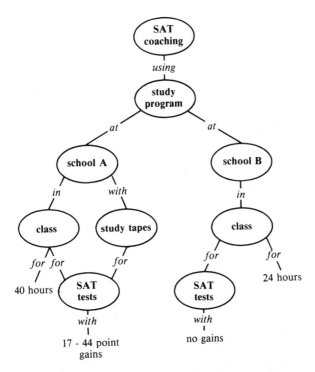

Figure 2.14 A concept map showing the key ideas in a journal article on the value of coaching for improving SAT scores (Sesnowitz et al. 1982).

We find that it is difficult to construct a complete concept map before beginning to write a paper (or chapter of a text). A first approximation can be prepared, however, which then can be quickly modified, added to, or reconstructed as the writing proceeds and the framework of ideas to be presented takes shape. Neither we nor our students have yet tried concept mapping for writing fiction, but we anticipate that the schematic nature of concept maps should provide the flexibility needed for fabricating interesting tales.

Written or spoken messages are necessarily *linear* sequences of concepts and propositions. In contrast, knowledge is stored in our minds in a kind of *hierarchical* or holographic structure. When we generate written or spoken sentences, we must transform information from a hierarchical to a linear structure. Conversely, when we read or hear messages, we must transform linear sequences into a

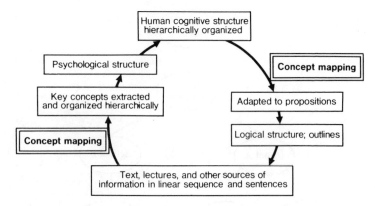

Figure 2.15 Schema illustrating how information is translated from or to the hierarchical structure of the brain to or from the linear structure of spoken or written language.

hierarchical structure in order to assimilate them into our minds. (See Figure 2.15) Concept mapping can aid this psychological–linguistic transformation, and more research is needed on how concept mapping can best be used to facilitate writing.

What has been said about writing papers applies also to the preparation of posters, handbill notices, exhibits, or mock-ups, and possibly to the construction of models as well (although we have not yet completed research on the latter). For a poster or exhibit, the concept mapping procedure might be carried over almost intact, with strings or ribbons tying together key ideas, pictures, or specimens to show hierarchical organization of meaning. We invite readers' comments on successes (or failures) that they experience using concept mapping to prepare papers or expositions.

3

THE VEE HEURISTIC FOR UNDERSTANDING KNOWLEDGE AND KNOWLEDGE PRODUCTION

WHY USE A HEURISTIC?

A HEURISTIC is something employed as an aid to solving a problem or understanding a procedure. The Vee heuristic was first developed to help students and instructors clarify the nature and purpose of laboratory work in science. It grew out of a twenty-year search by Gowin for a method to help students understand the structure of knowledge and the ways in which humans produce knowledge, and evolved from his "five questions" procedure, a scheme for "unpacking" the knowledge in any particular field.[1] Since 1977, when the Vee was first introduced to college students and teachers, it has been well received, and we have found it relevant in virtually every discipline represented at a university. In 1978 the heuristic was first introduced to junior high school students to help them "learn how to learn" science, and since then it has been applied as an aid to learning in many fields of study at both the secondary and college levels. One of the objectives of this book is to encourage expanded use and evaluation of the potential of the Vee heuristic.

In Chapter 1 (Figure 1.2) we presented a simple version of the Vee containing the key elements necessary to understand the nature of knowledge and knowledge production. Figure 3.1 shows a more complete Vee containing descriptions and other elements that can be considered. The heavy lines at the base of the Vee serve to emphasize that these are key elements that must be considered carefully in any inquiry. Concepts operate in an explicit way to select the events or objects we choose to observe and the records we choose to make.

---

1   Gowin's original five questions, to be applied to any document or exposition presenting knowledge, were (1) What is the "telling question"? (2) What are the key concepts? (3) What methods of inquiry (procedural commitments) are used? (4) What are the major knowledge claims? and (5) What are the value claims? (For more information, see Gowin 1970, 1972, 1980, 1981.)

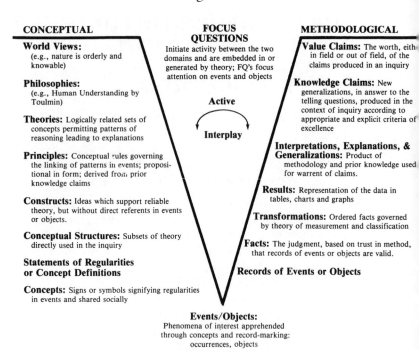

CONCEPTUAL

World Views:
(e.g., nature is orderly and knowable)

Philosophies:
(e.g., Human Understanding by Toulmin)

Theories: Logically related sets of concepts permitting patterns of reasoning leading to explanations

Principles: Conceptual rules governing the linking of patterns in events; propositional in form; derived from prior knowledge claims

Constructs: Ideas which support reliable theory, but without direct referents in events or objects.

Conceptual Structures: Subsets of theory directly used in the inquiry

Statements of Regularities or Concept Definitions

Concepts: Signs or symbols signifying regularities in events and shared socially

FOCUS QUESTIONS
Initiate activity between the two domains and are embedded in or generated by theory; FQ's focus attention on events and objects

Active

Interplay

METHODOLOGICAL

Value Claims: The worth, either in field or out of field, of the claims produced in an inquiry

Knowledge Claims: New generalizations, in answer to the telling questions, produced in the context of inquiry according to appropriate and explicit criteria of excellence

Interpretations, Explanations, & Generalizations: Product of methodology and prior knowledge used for warrent of claims.

Results: Representation of the data in tables, charts and graphs

Transformations: Ordered facts governed by theory of measurement and classification

Facts: The judgment, based on trust in method, that records of events or objects are valid.

Records of Events or Objects

Events/Objects:
Phenomena of interest apprehended through concepts and record-marking: occurrences, objects

Figure 3.1 An expanded version of Gowin's knowledge Vee with descriptions and examples of elements. In knowledge production or the interpretation of knowledge, all elements function interactively with each other to make sense out of the events or objects observed (see also Figure 1.2).

If our concepts are inadequate or faulty, our inquiry is already in difficulty. If our records are faulty, then we do not have *facts* (valid records) to work with and no form of transformation can lead to valid claims. The Vee helps us to see that although the meaning of all knowledge eventually derives from the events and/or objects we observe, there is nothing in the records of these events or objects that tells us what the records mean. This meaning must be constructed, and we must show how all elements interact when we construct new meanings.

In school science laboratories, students may be engrossed in making records of observations of events or objects, transforming these records into graphs, tables, or diagrams, and drawing conclusions, or *knowledge claims* – often without knowing why. Rarely do students deliberately invoke relevant concepts, principles, or theories in order to understand why specific events or objects have been chosen for observation, why they are making certain records or certain kinds of graphs or tables, or why their conclusions from the data are often "wrong," when judged against the textbook or other authority. In short, students' methodological or procedural activities are usually not consciously guided by the kinds of conceptual and theoretical ideas scientists use in their inquiries – there is no active interplay between the *thinking side* on the left of the Vee and the *doing side* on the right. As a result, science laboratory work is often frustrating and/or meaningless.

We see, then, that there is need for learning metaknowledge, or knowledge about how knowledge is produced. The Vee heuristic is a tool for acquiring knowledge about knowledge and how knowledge is constructed and used. As we noted in Chapter 1, there is a growing concern in education about the need for procedures to facilitate both metalearning and metaknowledge acquisition.

The construction of Vee diagrams, like the one shown in Figure 3.2, can help students grasp the meaning in laboratory work, and we have found that questions like the focus question asked there elicit good reflective thinking from our students. The Vee used as a heuristic with students helps them to see the interplay between what they already know and the new knowledge they are producing and attempting to understand. It should be evident that such a heuristic has psychological value because it not only encourages meaningful learning, but also helps learners to understand the process by which humans produce knowledge. The Vee heuristic deals with the nature of knowledge and the nature of learning in a complementary fashion. And when concept maps are explicitly used as part of the Vee, the link between knowledge and learning is even clearer.

Why a Vee-shaped heuristic? There is nothing sacred or absolute about it, but we have found the Vee shape to be valuable for several reasons. First, the Vee "points" to the events or objects that are at the root of all knowledge production, and it is crucial that learners become acutely aware of the events or objects they are experiencing, about which knowledge is to be constructed. Often this awareness is not present either in science laboratory work or work in other fields: For instance, what kind of events are we constructing when we consider the equation $2x + 6 = 10$? and what concepts and procedures lead us to claim that $x = 2$? Second, we have found that the Vee

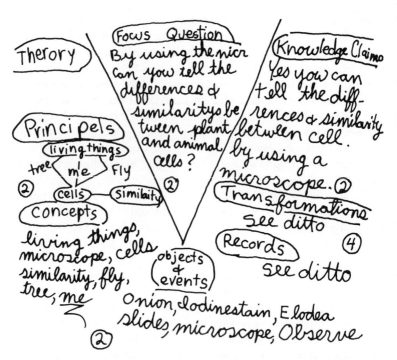

Figure 3.2 A Vee diagram dealing with lab work on cell study prepared by an "average" seventh-grade biology student guided by a dittoed work sheet. (The numbers in circles refer to points credited according to the scoring key shown in Table 3.3.)

shape helps students recognize the tension and interplay between disciplinary knowledge constructed (and modified) over time and the knowledge an inquiry allows them to construct here and now. Although the conceptual elements on the left side of the Vee illuminate our inquiry, these are constructions (conceptions) that have been developed over time, whereas the elements on the right are constructions for the immediate inquiry. Although it is true that new knowledge claims may lead to new concepts or even new theories, this is a process that is spread over years or decades in most disciplines.

Another value of the Vee form is that because inquiries often go awry right at the bottom of the Vee, it is less easy to ignore relevant key events or objects or key concepts. With the point of the Vee signal, one is less likely to gather the wrong records or to fail to see the meaning of the records that are gathered. A perfect example of this trouble occurs repeatedly in educational research when investigators fail to recognize that the test response marked by a student is a very constrained kind of record of that student's thinking. Educational researchers may proceed to total the number of items marked "correctly," perform elegant statistical transformations on the test scores, and then produce claims about the "learning" effectiveness demonstrated by some group, procedure, or ability. When in fact, no records of learning were made; no event of learning was observed. Whole sets of conceptual assumptions about the event of cognitive output that led to the student's marks on the test paper were simply ignored. Is it any wonder that educational research has produced so little functional knowledge in the past seventy-five years? (See Novak 1979b.) We will have more to say on the problems of learning evaluation in Chapters 7 and 8.

As time goes on and we continue to work with Gowin's Vee heuristic, we may find some other configural arrangement that is more powerful or more useful. This would be of no major consequence; heuristics have no absolute or inherent validity; their value accrues only from whatever usefulness they exhibit. Nevertheless, it is likely that each of the elements on the right and left sides of the Vee will be necessary in any heuristic.

INTRODUCING THE VEE TO STUDENTS

Management of learning in the classroom is never an easy task. When we attempt to achieve learning about knowledge (learning metaknowledge) we face problems that cut across all four of Schwab's commonplaces. The major problem involves governance: How do we get teachers and students to focus attention on acquiring metaknowledge? The Vee helps solve this governance problem, and also helps with curriculum design, by structuring educational experience in a way that requires that teacher and learner pay explicit attention to metaknowledge issues, whatever the specific context of the learning.

Our work with junior high school science students has shown that seventh graders are just as successful as eighth graders in acquiring and using the Vee heuristic. It is therefore reasonable to expect that at least upper elementary school students could be introduced to the heuristic, and we invite comments from elementary teachers who try the Vee. With students from grade seven on, we have found the same teaching strategies for introducing the Vee about equally effective, although younger students need more time to become familiar with its use. Though we are providing only one set of procedures, they include a variety of options that suggest how flexible approaches to teaching students how to understand and apply the Vee can be. Sample Vee maps from a variety of disciplines are shown in Appendix II.

Begin with concepts, objects, events. Concept mapping should be introduced before the Vee so that students are already familiar with two elements of the Vee: concepts, and the objects and/or events pertaining to them. The definition of concepts should be reviewed and a simple, familiar set of events chosen to illustrate them. For example, the regularities represented by the concepts water, melting, ice, steam, boiling, solid, liquid, and gas could be discussed with the students. No doubt many students will have some fuzzy meanings for one or more of these concepts, but the variation in meanings will be useful to illustrate why different people sometimes see different things when they observe the same object(s) or event(s).

Introduce the idea of records and focus questions. When we are involved in constructing knowledge, we use concepts we know to observe events or objects and make some form of *records* of our observations. The kind of records we make is also guided by one or more *focus questions:* Different focus questions lead us to focus on different aspects of the events or objects we are observing. Again using the water example, we could ask, What happens to the temperature of ice water as we apply heat? or How does the appearance of water change as it changes from ice to steam? In the Vee in Figure 3.3, we have chosen the first question as our focus question. When asked if additional concepts are needed to understand what is happening in the event being observed, some students might suggest steam, flame, and beaker or jar; others might cite more subtle concepts such as atoms, molecules, expansion (of mercury in the thermometer), temperature, or calories. The concepts of solid, liquid, and gas may also be applied. Students will begin to see that true understanding of an apparently simple event (heating ice water) can require the application of many concepts, some of which have relatively little meaning to them.

The obvious records to be kept in this example would be temper-

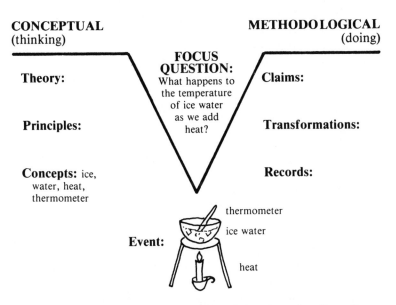

Figure 3.3 Sample Vee for constructing knowledge about the effect of heating on ice water.

atures, time, and changes in the amount of ice and water, but students should be asked for other suggestions, and then asked how they think these records might be organized or transformed.[2] Each student should construct a table for organizing the records and two or three students should illustrate their differing tables on the board.

Record transformation and knowledge claims. The purpose of transforming records is to organize our observations in a form that allows us to construct answers to our focus question. Students should discuss the different table formats suggested and decide which one(s) best organize observations to answer the focus question. There may be a suggestion that ideas from two or three different tables be combined. All this serves to show students that some of the creativity needed to construct new knowledge must be applied to finding the best way to organize observations. It should also become evident to

2 It is customary to use the term *data* for both the initial records and the transformed records. It is important that students recognize the difference between raw data (initial records) and the data in transformed records.

them that the combinations of concepts and principles we know influences how we design record transformations.

From our transformed data, we can begin to construct *knowledge claims* – claims about what we think the answer to our question should be. Knowledge claims are the products of an inquiry. Here again, it should be made evident to the students that constructing knowledge requires that we apply concepts and principles we already know. On the other hand, the process of constructing *new* knowledge allows us to enhance and/or alter the meanings of those concepts and principles, and to see new relationships between them. There is an active interplay between what we know and our new observations and knowledge claims. And this is how human cultures expand their understanding of both natural and people-made events or objects.[3]

Figure 3.4 shows records and a data table for the event of heating ice water. If this is the event chosen for observation, students can study the records and table and construct their own knowledge claims or answers to the focus question. The knowledge claims can be written on the blackboard and the students asked if they agree with each claim, or if not, why. This discussion should help illustrate that not everyone comes up with the same knowledge claims, that there may be disagreement among equally knowledgeable people on the validity of specific knowledge claims, and that knowledge claims are dependent on the kind of records we choose to make and the way we transform our data. The students can be shown the data in Table 3.1 and asked how their knowledge claims would differ with this information. Some students may recognize that the temperature remained fairly constant when water was changing from ice to liquid or liquid to gas, but they will probably not know the concepts, principles, or theory necessary to explain these observations.

Some students might suggest that we could further transform our observations by making a graph plotting water temperature against time. Graphs are a common form of record transformation in the natural and social sciences. Figure 3.5 shows a graph constructed from the information in Table 3.1. As students acquire more experience with the Vee heuristic, they could try to construct a variety of rec-

---

3 That other ways of predicting or interpreting events or objects – such as religion or clairvoyance – are possible and may come into the discussion, but we are concerned here with rational inquiry only.

The Vee heuristic for understanding knowledge

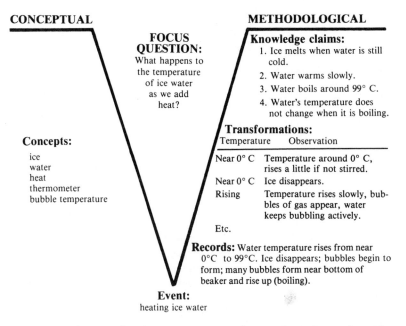

CONCEPTUAL

METHODOLOGICAL

FOCUS QUESTION:
What happens to the temperature of ice water as we add heat?

Knowledge claims:
1. Ice melts when water is still cold.
2. Water warms slowly.
3. Water boils around 99° C.
4. Water's temperature does not change when it is boiling.

Transformations:

Temperature	Observation
Near 0° C	Temperature around 0° C, rises a little if not stirred.
Near 0° C	Ice disappears.
Rising	Temperature rises slowly, bubbles of gas appear, water keeps bubbling actively.
Etc.	

Concepts:
ice
water
heat
thermometer
bubble temperature

Records: Water temperature rises from near 0°C to 99°C. Ice disappears; bubbles begin to form; many bubbles form near bottom of beaker and rise up (boiling).

Event:
heating ice water

Figure 3.4 The Vee showing concepts, records, transformed records, and knowledge claims for the event of heating ice water. More detailed records are shown in Table 3.1.

ord transformations for the same event, which could be a good test of their creativity as well as of their understanding of relevant concepts. The use of the Vee as an evaluation tool will be discussed in Chapter 6.

Principles and theories. On the left side of the Vee, above concepts, are *principles* and *theories*. Principles are significant relationships between two or more concepts that guide our understanding of the significant action in the events studied. For example, the principle "Pure water boils at 100° C at sea level" describes a specific relationship between the boiling point of a pure substance (water) at a given atmospheric pressure (sea level or 760 mm of mercury). Principles come from knowledge claims produced by inquiries over time, and they in turn guide the observation of events or objects and the transformation of records in subsequent inquiries. Principles are something scholars in a discipline construct, and students of a discipline

Table 3.1. *One example of transformed data for the event of heating water*

Time	Temperature	Observation
10:00	1° C	Ice is floating near top of beaker.
10:05	3° C	Ice water is a little warmer.
10:06	1° C	Water temperature goes down after ice water is stirred.
10:10	2° C	Most of the ice is melted.
10:12	8° C	Ice is gone; water temperature is rising; small bubbles appear on side of jar.
10:14	30° C	Water temperature is rising.
10:16	51° C	Water temperature is rising.
10:18	71° C	Water temperature is rising.
10:22	98° C	Water temperature is rising; small bubbles on sides are gone; bubbles begin to appear at bottom of beaker.
10:23	99° C	Large bubbles rise from bottom of beaker.
10:28	99° C	Water temperature is constant; water is boiling.

may eventually understand. In ordinary science laboratory work, students are often not explicitly aware of the principles that might be guiding their inquiry, and it is useful to spend some time identifying one or more principles relevant to an inquiry, although this is difficult if one is not thoroughly familiar with the discipline. For example, in addition to the principle relating the boiling point of water and air pressure, other principles relevant to our example would be density (ice is less dense than water and floats; warm water is less dense than cold and rises), diffusion and convection (which account for the small rise in temperature and the drop after stirring), and energy conservation (heat energy is being transferred to the ice water). Even a simple event can be enormously complex, depending on how far we wish to go in the range and precision of the observations we make and the subsequent knowledge claims we choose to construct.

Theories are similar to principles in that they explain relationships between concepts, but they organize concepts and principles in order

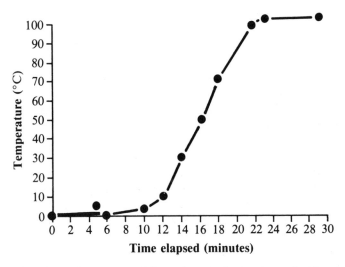

Figure 3.5 A graph constructed from the experiment shown in Figure 3.4 and the data in Table 3.1.

to describe events and claims about events. Theories are usually regarded as broader and more inclusive than principles and may encompass dozens of specific concepts and principles. Thus, the cell theory in biology and the kinetic molecular theory in physical science are broad explanatory ideas that subsume hundreds of more specific relationships. This makes theories powerful for guiding inquiries, but it also accounts for why theories are difficult to understand. Even specialists in a field may differ in their understanding of a theory, but they all use the theory as best they can to design studies and/or to explain their observations. Principles tell us *how* events or objects appear or behave, whereas theories tell us *why* they do so.

Because they are broad and comprehensive by nature, there are relatively few theories in each discipline. It usually takes a genius to construct a substantially new theory, and most disciplines have only a few geniuses per century. People like Newton, Darwin, and Einstein in the sciences and Mozart and Bach in music are very rare. Even Bach and Mozart never actually propounded new theories of music, although they did significantly alter the scope and richness of musical events through their creative works. In general, though theories in different domains of human understanding – science, literature, mathematics, philosophy – take on somewhat different structures, they all represent broad, inclusive standards of meaning and excellence in those fields.

In spite of their somewhat elusive nature, theories should not be ignored, and whenever possible students should be helped to see the theories operating in any inquiry. For instance, kinetic molecular theory would be relevant to the water and ice experiment, and it could be explained to the students if they (and the teacher) are sufficiently conversant with the structures of science.

Value claims. Up to this point, our attention has been focused on the knowledge elements of the Vee. We have found that with many groups of students, it is best to delay discussion of value claims until they are familiar and comfortable with knowledge claims. There is always an affective or feeling component in knowledge and value claims, and the feelings can sometimes be intensely positive or negative (as with claims about tobacco, drugs, or sex). Value claims give answers to value questions such as, Is this any good? or bad? What is it good for? Is it right? Ought we choose it? Can we make it better? In our two examples, the claims one could make are not likely to have emotional valence.

In the Vee on water and ice, we could suggest such value claims as, It is good to avoid unnecessary freezing and thawing to save energy. Or, Wasting hot water is a misuse of energy. For the learning example described in the next section, we could give value claims such as, Learners will benefit from help in identifying concepts in learning tasks. Or, Success in learning should be encouraged through awareness of relevant concepts students possess that can facilitate learning. Or, apropos of this book, It is good to teach students how to utilize metalearning strategies.

Knowledge claims and value claims are not independent. Gowin (1981) suggests that knowledge claims and value claims "ride in the same boat, but they are not the same passenger." There is an interrelationship, but there is also a distinction, and it is important to stress this judgment. Discussions with students can help them see both the philosophical uniqueness of value claims and knowledge claims and their dependence on each other. Further discussion of value claims is included in Chapters 6 and 8.

The Vee heuristic for understanding knowledge

One of the reasons the natural sciences developed earlier and progressed further than the social sciences is that events or objects in the natural sciences are usually easier to isolate and observe carefully, and have more universal regularities, which makes it easier to discern the regularities and to invent concepts to represent them. But, as we saw in the water and ice example, even seemingly simple natural phenomena can become enormously complex as the relevant concepts we apply become more numerous, allowing us to consider new regularities that were not at first manifested. The social sciences, in their current "primitive" state, may therefore provide even simpler examples than the natural sciences to illustrate how humans construct knowledge.

For this example, we have chosen as our events for observation the recall success of students performing five learning activities. The focus question here might be stated as, How many chunks of information can students recall after a brief learning exposure? The events we construct are brief exposures (5 to 10 seconds) to the following groups of items to be recalled:

(1) 8 13 21 5 11 18 26 3 12 7
(2) Q C V V M E P Y T O
(3) pet dog cat mouse rabbit turtle fish animal house door
(4) petunia gardenia marigold zinnia goldenrod sunflower
    maple sycamore cottonwood walnut
(5) tracheid xylem cambium phloem epidermis palisade
    mesophyll stomate aperture plastid

Each list contains 10 items, but the lists are significantly different in terms of the meaning they contain. Figure 3.6 shows a Vee diagram constructed for this learning experiment as it might be presented to students. A few relevant concepts are listed; more should be added as the discussion proceeds. The class should discuss how the focus question and the events are related.

This set of events can be recreated right in the classroom, and each student can make his or her own records for the learning events. One or more overhead transparencies should be made so that each of the five lists of items can be exposed separately. Each list is presented for 10 seconds, then covered. (A longer or shorter interval can be chosen if there are several classes and the results compared by class.) Students should write down all the items they can recall. Expose the list

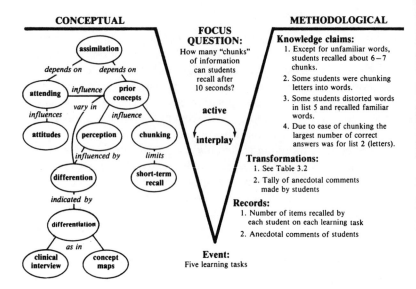

Figure 3.6 A sample Vee for the example on learning events involving five recall tasks. A concept map represents the "thinking" side of the Vee.

and have them record and then score the number of items they could remember, and keep this as a record. Proceed in the same way for the other four lists. Now each student has a record of the number of items recalled for each of the five lists.

Students can now be asked to suggest ways to transform the records so that they would be easier to use to answer the focus question. Two or three different table formats might be suggested and placed on the blackboard so that the merits of each as it relates to the focus question and the concepts listed can be discussed. Again, it is important to note that there is no one *best* way to transform data; different transformations may lead to different knowledge claims. Table 3.2 shows one possible table format for these records.

Some knowledge claims can now be constructed with the students, and the students can discuss how these claims can be explained in terms of the concepts they know. This may be a good time to bring in George Miller's (1956) idea of a *chunk*. We cannot retain in short-term memory more than about seven chunks of information. The size of each chunk, however, depends on knowledge we have in long-term memory. Words are usually stored whole, so that even

Table 3.2. *Transformed records for the five learning events showing number of students and number of elements recalled for each task*

Task	Number of students recalling elements											Total correct answers
	0	1	2	3	4	5	6	7	8	9	10	
1	0	0	0	0	2	6	7	11	5	1	0	206
2	0	0	0	0	1	3	7	4	9	8	4	273
3	0	0	0	0	1	2	7	8	8	4	3	254
4	0	1	3	4	5	4	6	8	4	1	0	136
5	1	4	11	14	5	1	0	0	0	0	0	94

though 7 words contain more bits of information (letters), we can usually remember 7 familiar words as easily as 7 short numbers or 7 independent letters. (Our data showed that many students could recall all 10 letters in list 2, which seemed to defy the principle that short-term memory can only store about 7 chunks until some students told us they "chunked" the last 6 letters as "me pyto," and hence had only the first 4 letters plus 2 chunks to recall.) The students should now discuss the strategies they used to learn and recall each of the five tasks and relate these strategies to the concepts and claims on the Vee.

Miller's principle of chunking and the 7 (plus or minus 2) chunks that most of us can hold in short-term memory is a relevant principle for this inquiry. The study also shows that we can recall familiar words more easily than unfamiliar words, and therefore that word meanings and spellings influence chunk size. Even though the words in both lists 4 and 5 are about plants, the words in list 5 are probably unfamiliar to most students (unless they recently studied botany).

We can also see from this study that there is an interplay between perception and long-term information store. The unfamiliar words in list 5 surely were not easy for students to "read" because they could not relate some or most of these words to concepts they already knew. They probably recognized each as a valid word and perhaps read them as words; however, without the word–concept meaning linkage, they may have distorted some of the words and/or "recalled" different words that looked similar and for which they had established meanings. This principle of distorting our perceptions according to what we know (or believe or have strong feelings about) is well established and is a source of much difficulty in courtrooms, where different witnesses often report that they saw different things in the same accident or crime event (see, for example, Rodgers 1982).

We can apply either information processing theory or Ausubelian learning theory in this inquiry. The choice, however, will influence further transformation of the records and also the kind of claims we make – another case where theory, when deliberately applied, can influence our claims, which in turn can add new meaning to our understanding of the theory. Just how choosing information processing versus Ausubelian theory would influence our knowledge construction in this example is unfortunately too complex an argument to take up here.

As we have noted, a concept map is one way to present the lower left, or thinking side of the Vee. With many events, students are likely to experience considerable difficulty in constructing a concept map to present the thinking side of the Vee. This, of course, is one reason students have difficulty understanding laboratory or field work. Building a good concept map is always a challenging task and teachers should plan on having to do a certain amount of negotiating to achieve shared meaning. It is often frightening to venture into tasks where uncertainty abounds, but these are also experiences from which much learning can occur. The left side of the Vee in Figure 3.6 is an example of a concept map that could represent the thinking side of the Vee in our learning example.

SCORING VEE DIAGRAMS

As with concept maps, it is possible to construct scoring keys to assign numerical values to Vee diagrams. Table 3.3 shows one scoring key we developed for use in a research project with junior high school science students, and an example of scoring is shown in Figure 3.2. The points assigned for any aspect of a Vee are arbitrary, and the set of values we suggest for each element (from 0 to 3 or 4 points) is only one of any number of variations. In practice, more weight could be given to one or two aspects of the Vee considered to be more important either because of the type of material being analyzed or to emphasize acquisition of particular skills; the focus question, relevant principles, or other elements might even receive two or three times the number of score points assigned to the others.

Table 3.3. *Scoring key for Vee diagrams, developed for use with junior high school science students*

Focus question

0–No focus question is identified.

1–A question is identified, but does not focus upon the objects and the major event OR the conceptual side of the Vee.

2–A focus question is identified; includes concepts, but does not suggest objects or the major event OR the wrong objects and event are identified in relation to the rest of the laboratory exercise.

3–A clear focus question is identified; includes concepts to be used and suggests the major event and accompanying objects.

Objects/event

0–No objects or event are identified.

1–The major event OR the objects are identified and are consistent with the focus question, OR an event and objects are identified, but are inconsistent with the focus question.

2–The major event with accompanying objects is identified, and is consistent with the focus question.

3–Same as above, but also suggests what records will be taken.

Theory, principles, and concepts

0–No conceptual side is identified.

1–A few concepts are identified, but without principles and theory, or a principle written is the knowledge claim sought in the laboratory exercise.

2–Concepts and at least one type of principle (conceptual or methodological) OR concepts and relevant theory are identified.

3–Concepts and two types of principles are identified, OR concepts, one type of principle, and a relevant theory are identified.

4–Concepts, two types of principles, and a relevant theory are identified.

Records/transformations

0–No records or transformations are identified.

1–Records are identified, but are inconsistent with the focus question or the major event.

2–Records OR transformations are identified, but not both.

3–Records are identified for the major event; transformations are inconsistent with the intent of the focus question.

4–Records are identified for the major event; transformations are consistent with the focus question and the grade level and ability of the student.

Table 3.3. *(cont.)*

Knowledge claim
    0–No knowledge claim is identified.
    1–Claim is ~~unrelated to~~ the left-hand side of the Vee.
    2–Knowledge claim includes a concept used in an improper context OR
        a generalization that is inconsistent with the records and
        transformations.
    3–Knowledge claim includes the concepts from the focus question and
        is derived from the records and transformations.
    4–Same as above, but the knowledge claim leads to a new focus
        question.

A simple method for scoring Vees constructed from expository material would be to assign 0 to 10 points for answers to each of the ten questions given in the next section. Scores would vary from perhaps 50 or less to 100 and could be presented as a percent of the maximum score (100). Because students are used to percentage scores, these scores tell them quickly how well (or poorly) they have done. Another way to use the scoring key in Table 3.3 would be to award 2 bonus points for each of the 10 elements of the Vee shown on well-done diagrams, for a total of 20 possible points. (Multiplying points earned by 5 would convert map scores into percentages.) When students are asked to construct a concept map to present the left side of the Vee, then the scoring criteria for concepts maps can be merged into the scoring key for Vees.

The actual assessment of responses for each element of the Vee does require some judgment. We have found high concordance among judges' scores for the same Vee diagrams. As one develops and uses one's own scoring criteria, scoring becomes relatively easy, consistent, and reasonably objective. As with concept maps, we must be cognizant of creative alternatives and retain some flexibility in scoring Vees. More research is needed on the effects of alternative procedures for scoring Vees.

THE VEE APPLIED TO READING MATERIAL

Experiments or other constructed events are not the only places where the Vee can be used constructively; it has also proven to be a valuable heuristic when applied to reading material.

The Vee heuristic for understanding knowledge

The most directly relevant application is in the critical reading of research papers (in any field). Research papers always purport to make some knowledge claims in the discipline(s) to which they are directed. Hence, we can "lay the Vee" on these papers and ask questions such as

(1) What objects and/or events were being observed?
(2) What records or record transformations were made?
(3) What was/were the focus question(s)?
(4) What relevant concepts or principles were cited or implied?
(5) Do the records made validly record the main aspects of the events and/or objects observed?
(6) Are relevant principles stated, implied, or ignored?
(7) What theory was stated or implied in the research, if any?
(8) Is there a conscious, deliberate effort to tie concepts and principles to the (a) events and/or objects observed, (b) records made, (c) record transformations, and (d) knowledge claims?
(9) Were any value claims made, and if so, are they congruent with the knowledge claims?
(10) Was there a better focus question, or do the results answer a focus question other than what was (or can be inferred to have been) stated?

Surely the above questions make clear that the Vee heuristic can help to "dissect" the meaning and value of a research report (and this statement is a value claim). Waterman and Rissler (1982) have shown some ways to apply the Vee to scientific literature. We have found that most research reports fail on some or all of the above criteria. Is it any wonder that there is so much debate regarding what we know about any event or set of events? Take, for example, the shutdown of the nuclear power plant at Three Mile Island, the Vietnam War, or the Democratic Party losses in the 1980 elections. Knowledge making is a very elusive business. Anyone who claims to have *the* answers to complex events is probably either being foolish or deceptive (and this, too, is a value claim as well as a knowledge claim).

Some of the Vees our students have constructed from reading materials are reproduced in Appendix 2. Given the many disciplines or fields of inquiry – to say nothing about the variety of concerns in any one field – it is evident that these samples reflect only a fraction of a percent in the range of possible Vees, and of the knowledge and value claims made by human beings. We hope this book will stimulate application and analysis of claims in a much wider and more diverse range of rational human intellectual activities.

APPLICATION OF THE VEE TO INSTRUCTIONAL
PLANNING FOR LABORATORY OR STUDIO WORK

In Chapter 1, we said that the Vee heuristic had its primary origins in our efforts to analyze why scientific laboratory work was judged by scientists to be valuable. Since the Vee was first proposed in 1977, we have found the heuristic to be useful in many contexts other than scientific laboratory work, although it remains a powerful tool in the sciences.

We have found that applying the Vee heuristic to the analysis of descriptions in laboratory study guides can reveal conceptual gaps not only in the laboratory notes and/or descriptions of observations, but also in the "backgrounding," or description of how an experiment or observation fits into the conceptual matrix of concerns in the field. Key concepts or other factors often are missing, and the same ten questions asked for written research reports can be applied to laboratory guide instructions. Chen (1980) and Buchweitz (1981) both found that student successes or failures in physics laboratories could probably be linked to the adequacy or inadequacy of laboratory guide instructions.

In the sciences and other fields, it is common to find that a given exercise does not produce the desired understandings. After some attempts to "try this or try that," troublesome activity is often scrapped and a new activity substituted. But behold, the same difficulties encountered in the original activity are often manifest in the new one! How can we break out of this? We suggest two ways.

First, as Chen (1980) and Buchweitz (1981) have shown, study guides can be analyzed, defects located, learning problems identified, and corrections made in a systematic way, and not just by employing "blood, guts, and intuition." We do not disparage the use of the latter, but experience has shown us over the years that the insights of competent scholars and teachers are not good enough to solve teaching and learning problems. Something more is needed. We suggest that Vee diagramming of activities can be a valuable additional teaching tool.

Second, students are often not aware of their lack of understanding or misunderstanding of exercises. They are often willing to accept wildly erroneous answers without questioning why or how such claims could be valid. They seldom test their conclusions (which we prefer to call claims) against those that relevant concepts or principles would suggest, or even against common sense. Thus we may find students claiming that a man could lift 2,000 pounds 3 feet and thus do 6,000 foot-pounds of work, which surely stretches credibility if one stops to think about it. But then, in meaningless school learning, who would expect answers to lab or test problems to make sense?

What we have said about laboratory work applies in many ways to studio work or performances in art, music, sculpture, sports, architecture, and so on. As we have had only limited experience in these areas, we cannot yet cite persuasive studies (although studies in fields other than science and social science are in progress).

The Vee is also a useful heuristic for the design of instructional programs. Whether a single laboratory or studio activity or an entire four-year curriculum for college students is being designed, the Vee heuristic can help to define the knowledge to be included (or excluded) in the program of instruction and also help to suggest alternative pedagogical strategies. This use of the Vee will be discussed further in Chapter 4.

We conclude this chapter as we did the last on concept mapping, by inviting our readers to explore for themselves how these heuristic devices can best be employed with students in a variety of contexts and fields. We are confident that the learning theory and philosophy of knowledge guiding our work is valid. What is needed is more application, testing, evaluating, and analysis to fulfill the promise and assess the limitations of these heuristic devices.

4

NEW STRATEGIES FOR
INSTRUCTIONAL PLANNING

THIS CHAPTER will illustrate strategies for using concept mapping and Vee diagramming for planning a total curriculum program (e.g., a B.S. degree in social work) as well as specific instructional activities (e.g., tomorrow's lesson in math). All too often, educational theory is of no help when it comes to planning tomorrow's lesson. We will try to illustrate how concept mapping and Vees can help educators design not only their next lesson, but their total instructional program as well.

We will sketch only a few of the potential uses of these ideas for instructional planning. We hope that readers will venture beyond our examples and test, evaluate, and criticize the application of these strategies in other areas of educating, and we would welcome communication with educators about successes or difficulties.

THE USES OF CONCEPT MAPPING

For major curriculum planning, concept mapping is the key pedagogical strategy we wish to advance. As indicated in Chapter 2, it is possible to organize concept maps either for an entire educational program or for part of a simple lesson. It is necessary to use a variety of levels of concept inclusiveness: broad, integrative concepts should be the basis for planning the curriculum for a given course of study, whereas more specific, less inclusive concepts serve as guidelines for selecting specific instructional materials and activities. Put another way, top of a disciplinary concept map guides major curriculum planning activities, whereas the lower portion implies specific instructional activities, including the specific events or objects to be studied. Figure 4.1 shows schematically how concept maps apply to curriculum and instructional planning. Good curriculum planning requires deciding on 4 to 7[1] concepts that are central to understanding the discipline, or segment of it, under consideration. Instructional planning involves slicing vertically through the curriculum map to achieve meaningful linkages between more general, inclusive concepts and more specific concepts. As instruction proceeds, conceptual cross links will be needed, and these would be represented by horizontal lines across the curriculum conceptual hierarchy. Students need to be encouraged to make such cross links, and to see how nearly all new concepts can be related to previously learned concepts.

There is no best way to represent subject matter on a concept map. Most teachers plan their program around one or more textbooks, so the starting point would be to map the section or chapter under consideration. Figure 4.2 shows four alternative ways to make concept maps for one chapter of a high school biology textbook. The maps differ in detail, but all four contain the same key concepts presented in the chapter. Not shown in these concept maps are cross links to other chapters or units; to illustrate concept maps for each of twenty or so chapters would obviously require much more space than one or two pages of this book. As we suggested in Chapter 2, however, it is possible to place chapter or unit concept maps around the walls of a classroom to provide the visual props needed for continuous cross referencing of key concepts.

Outlines and concept maps. Most textbooks, lectures, and other expository materials are planned from outlines. Outlines and concept maps differ in three important ways. First, good concept maps show key concepts and propositions in very explicit and concise language. Outlines usually intermix instructional examples, concepts, and propositions in a matrix that may be hierarchical, but fails to show the superordinate–subordinate relationship between key concepts and propositions. Second, good concept maps are concise, and show the key ideational relationship in a simple visual fashion that uses the remarkable human capability for visual imagery. Many of our students report that they can recall "seeing" how two or more propositions were related on a concept map. Finally, concept maps visually

1 One of the reasons we suggest limiting the number of concepts at any level of a concept hierarchy is that people can only deal with at most 7 or 8 ideas simultaneously (Miller 1956, Simon 1974). Allowing some "chunk space" for procedural ideas, 3 or 4 concepts at any level of a concept map are probably optimal for learning.

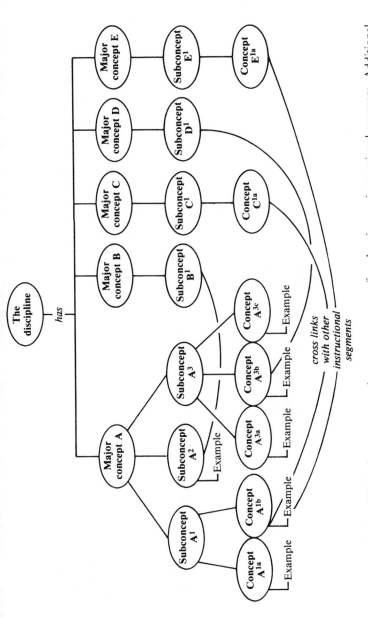

Figure 4.1 A simplified schema representing a concept map for planning an instructional program. Additional subordinate concepts and cross links, along with specific examples, would be included in a complete plan.

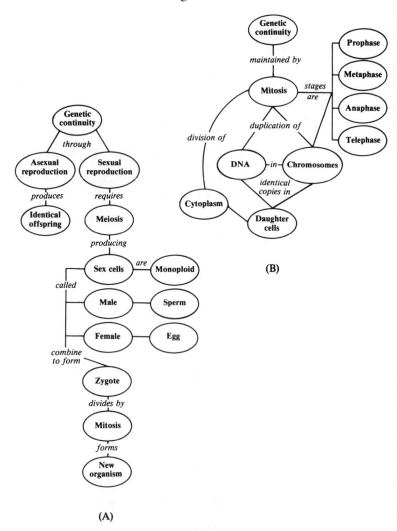

(B)

(A)

Figure 4.2 Four concept maps constructed to illustrate the major propositions in Chapter 6 of Oram, Hummer, and Smoot (1979). The maps show alternative hierarchies constructed from the key concepts in the chapter. We have added the superordinate concept, genetic continuity.

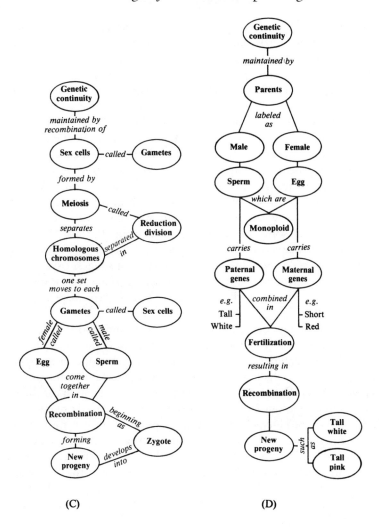

(C)

(D)

emphasize both hierarchical relationships between concepts and propositions and cross links between sets of concepts and propositions. Cross referencing is of course possible in outlines, but these do not have the dramatic visual impact of concept maps.

Concept maps and outlines both serve useful purposes, and we are not recommending that course outlines should be abandoned. On the contrary, we see the need for an active interplay between outlining and concept mapping. As noted in Chapter 2, our minds seem to work hierarchically to hold a matrix of interrelated concepts, but instruction is necessarily linear in form (We must present knowledge segment A, then segment B, then segment C, and so on.) Concept maps can help us to organize the whole set of concept–propositional relationships we wish to present, but we must then reduce this organization to some sequence of topic A, topic B, topic C, and so on. Concept maps do not specify the exact sequence for presentation, but they do show hierarchies of ideas that suggest psychologically valid sequences. Choosing the best linear sequence for instruction based on the hierarchical framework of concept maps requires artistic skill.

Most of the raw materials we use in curriculum and instructional planning are linear written or oral sequences of knowledge. Outlining this raw material can be a useful first step to concept mapping (or Vee making which will be discussed in the section on the uses of Gowin's Vee). We must recognize the need to go from linear didactic material → to outlines → to concept maps → to new organization of materials into hierachical concept maps → to outlines for instruction. Briefly, we are suggesting an instructional planning sequence that moves from linear text and/or outlines to hierarchical concept maps and back to linear didactic materials. Of course, the interposed concept maps can help students see greater meaning in each of the component concepts and recognize the relationships between them (Melby-Robb 1982).

Concept maps, because of their conciseness and visual imagery, can be much more helpful than outlines for planning an entire course (or major segment of instruction). We can look at the concept map for a whole course of study (this may cover the wall of a room) and see patterns and relationships of ideas immediately. This is not so easy with course outlines, if it can be done at all. Using the road map analogy again, we can see at a glance the major roads linking ideas, or we can look more closely and see the detailed propositional terrain we need to travel. Thus, concept mapping provides a visual image of the "big picture," as well as of the concept relationships in small instructional segments. Placed on large pieces of cardboard and perhaps drawn with colored felt pens, a "concept road map" can be of immediate and lasting value to students as imagery (Figure 4.3 is an example of such a map constructed for a course in history.)

AN EXAMPLE OF CURRICULUM DEVELOPMENT IN SCIENCE AND TECHNOLOGY

In 1974, we began a project aimed at developing a training program for scientists and engineers concerned with wastewater disposal. Rising energy costs and higher standards for wastewater treatment, together with water shortages in some areas, were making more feasible the age-old technique of using land to treat wastewater. The U.S. Environmental Protection Agency (EPA) and the Army Corps of Engineers were interested in a training program for civil and sanitary engineers and agency personnel to familiarize them with the promise and limitations of land treatment of wastewater and sewage sludges. With joint funding from the EPA and the Corps, an interdisciplinary project was begun with the cooperation of the departments of agricultural engineering, education, and agronomy at Cornell University.

The project faced two major tasks. First, there were no textbooks on land application treatment of wastewater and much of the relevant technical literature was distributed over many fields and journals in agronomy and engineering. Somehow this vast array of diverse knowledge had to be brought together and reduced to a curriculum plan for a one- or two-week training program appropriate for the audience. Second, it was necessary to accommodate participants with widely varying backgrounds, interests, experience, and training, and hence a modular, self-paced, flexible program was needed. Initially it was thought that the education department staff would advise on teaching techniques and audio-visual aids, whereas the staff from the agricultural engineering and agronomy departments would guide all other aspects of program development. As the project evolved, it was clear that the strategies professors commonly use to organize their courses were not going to be successful for collecting knowledge and

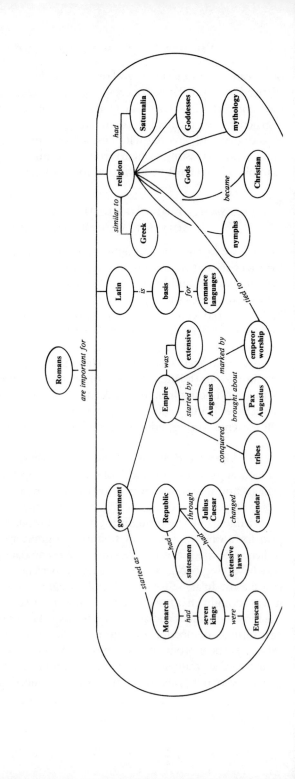

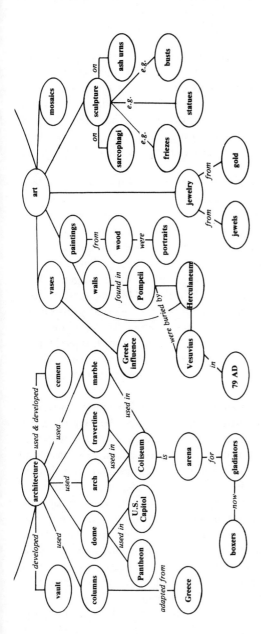

Figure 4.3 A concept map constructed to represent key ideas for a secondary school course in history. Additional topics could be added and corresponding concept map segments incorporated.

organizing this new multidisciplinary course. As matters worked out, no substantial progress was made in writing the instructional modules until concept mapping was adopted for organizing the overall curriculum and the individual study modules. Education expertise played a major role in selecting and organizing the content, as well as the construction, of specific learning aids, although the scientific and engineering expertise was also essential in the development of the program.

Our Land Application of Wastewater project thus faced problems in the categories of both curriculum and instruction. The primary constraints we needed to consider were that the training program must be usable over a short intensive interval (in practice, workshops of four and a half days were recommended) or through self-study, and that it must meet the needs of a diverse group. This constraint led to the decision to use a printed modular[2] format together with audio-tutorial units (Postlethwait, Novak, and Murray 1972), supplemented in workshops with lecturers, tutorial aid, and group problem-solving sessions. Our instructional strategies therefore departed substantially from traditional training programs, which typically offer a day-long series of lectures, some technical manuals or reprints of articles prepared for other purposes, and group question-and-answer sessions.

It took us almost a year of active work and meetings to reach a general consensus on the instructional format and the overall amount of content coverage we could expect to achieve given the nature of the audience. Part of this time was used to familiarize project staff members with the nature of meaningful learning and the role concepts play in it, and with the instructional strategies of modular and audio-tutorial teaching. Any group attempting interdisciplinary curriculum development should anticipate a time table of one to two years to achieve close integration of knowledge and new instructional strategies. Concept mapping and Vee making strategies facilitate this process. Once we began to devise concept maps, the total curriculum plan for our program was elucidated within a few weeks. Figure 4.4 is an example of the concept maps we prepared.

Preparation of written and audio-tutorial modules accelerated significantly once we had developed the concept maps for each of the

2 Modular instruction usually uses ideas from Bloom's (1968, 1976) "mastery learning" program wherein each module is relatively self-contained and gives explicit descriptions of learning goals keyed to study materials.

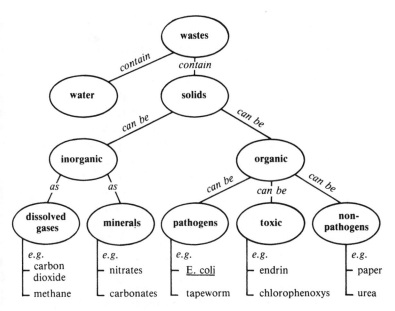

Figure 4.4 Example of a concept map prepared for the development of a modular instruction unit in a training program on wastewater treatment (adapted from Loehr et al. 1979).

planned twenty-one modules. Posted on a large bulletin board in the workroom for the project, the concept maps provided easy reference to the concepts and propositions that were to be presented in all units, thus making it possible to organize better the detailed content for any module. The module concept maps encouraged cross referencing of key ideas, and at the same time permitted the development of the comprehensive meaning intrinsic in each module.

The program was evaluated during its development in trial workshops, and later by groups, college classes, and individuals, and the response was highly positive. We were somewhat surprised at the high ratings for the audio-tutorial modules, since very few users were familiar with this approach.

The whole program was subsequently published (Loehr et al. 1979), and it stands, so far as we know, as the only published example of an instructional plan developed around concept maps.

Learning how to learn

Any educator who wishes to construct an instructional program from primary source materials faces the problem of converting disciplinary knowledge into a pedagogically usable form. The research studies, historical accounts, poems or novels, or musical scores constructed by creative scholars are usually not in a form such that new ideas they contain can be grasped easily by novice learners. As noted in Chapter 3, this problem of "unpacking" knowledge from the form in which it is presented by disciplinary experts into a one suitable for instruction has been a continuing concern. Since 1977, we have found Gowin's Vee to be an especially useful tool for analyzing original papers or other creative works to render them suitable for instructional planning. The Vee supplements and complements concept mapping as a strategy for curriculum planning and has been proven effective with a wide variety of source materials.

Analyzing original materials. The final product of any creative scholar's work does not reveal the false starts, the frameworks of alternative ideas tested, or the key concept linkages or propositions that guided the creative act (see, for example, Ghiselin 1952). Applying the Vee to this process of "unpacking" original work is an attempt to reconstruct the ideational and procedural frameworks that led to the creative product, thus unmasking the kind of thinking needed to understand how the final claims were generated from more or less commonplace events or objects. Often creative people are not consciously aware of the specific concepts or procedures and the interplay among them that led to new insight. Sometimes they can describe the process after the fact, but this is usually a "cleaned up" version that obscures the complexity of the creative process. Watson's (1968) book on the elucidation of the structure of DNA illustrates how convoluted the creative process can be.

What is the value of gaining insight into the creative process of knowledge production? The primary benefit is that we are better able to select content for inclusion in instruction and to order its sequence. Because the amount of potentially relevant information from which to select examples on any topic is unlimited, we must choose what to include and what to ignore. Vee making, particularly when used in conjunction with concept mapping, simplifies the problem of sequencing instruction because it makes clear what concepts or principles are needed to make sense out of the objects or events being studied, and what relevant concepts and principles must be subsequently introduced as records and record transformations are presented. There is, of course, no one ideal sequence for teaching anything; student cognitive frameworks are too idiosyncratic to allow such an ideal. Rather, every student must construct his or her meaning for a segment of knowledge (or else learn by rote) and a Vee diagram can serve as a kind of blueprint to aid teacher and/or student in this knowledge construction.

Improving laboratory, field, and studio instruction. To illustrate how the Vee can help, we cite again the work of Chen and Buchweitz. Figure 4.5 is a Vee diagram that Chen (1980) constructed from the laboratory guide for one of the exercises (on kinematics) in an introductory college physics course. Chen found that students in the course (1) did not understand the concept of coefficient of friction, (2) did not understand why they had to reduce the separation between gates by $\Delta x/2$ to measure the Δt for the bar on the glider to pass the second gate, (3) could not distinguish between average velocity and instantaneous velocity; they thought $\Delta x/\Delta t$ is $(x_2 - x_1)$ over $(t_2 - t_1)$ or x/t, and (4) got a slope close to 1 for the acceleration vs. θ graph without realizing that it should 980 cm/S^2 or close to 1,000 cm/S^2. Chen's Vee analysis of the guide showed (1) the key questions were not clearly given, hence students were not sure why they were making the specific observations; (2) the main objectives of the lab should have included study of the relationships between $x, v, t,$ and acceleration because these relationships are derived from graphing and are significant for comprehending the concept of constantly accelerated motion; (3) initial velocity equal to zero was given without any reason; (4) the concept of coefficient of friction, although it was to be taught later, was needed in this lab; (5) the explanation of reducing the gate separation by $x/2$ was obscure, and the adjustment is trivial; (6) some terms in the instructions were vague (e.g., the term velocity). From the Vee analysis, Chen found that some needed concepts were not included, or their relevance to the experiment not made clear, in the original instructions. Furthermore, the instructions did not clearly explain how the data gathered and the data transformations made related to concepts and principles and to the key questions. Chen rewrote the laboratory instructions so as to reduce or eliminate the deficiencies. As a result, there was very substantial

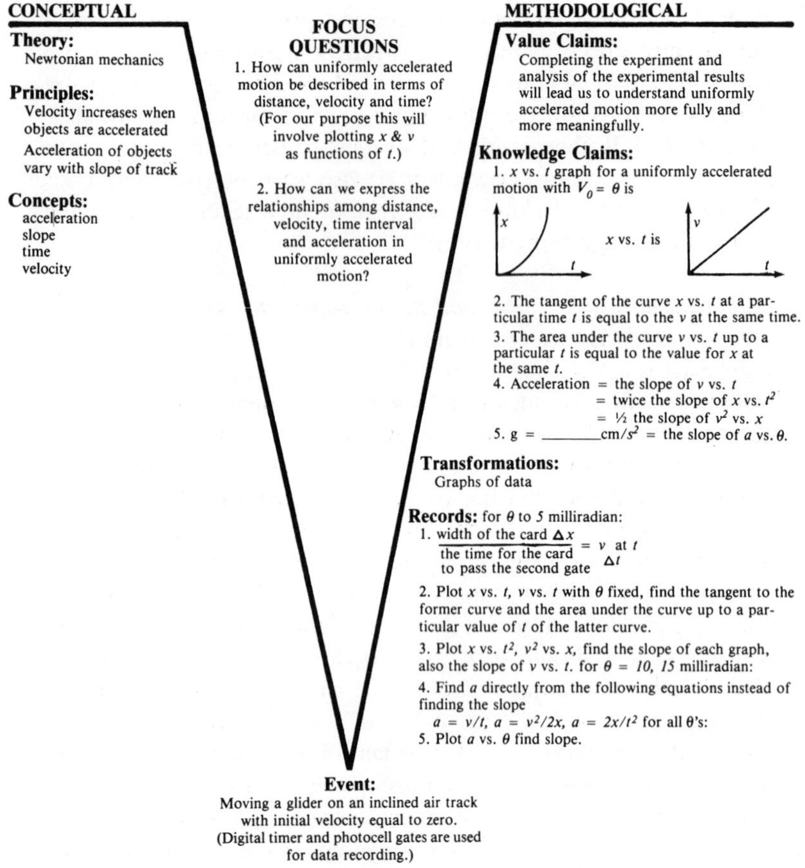

CONCEPTUAL

Theory:
Newtonian mechanics

Principles:
Velocity increases when objects are accelerated
Acceleration of objects vary with slope of track

Concepts:
acceleration
slope
time
velocity

FOCUS QUESTIONS

1. How can uniformly accelerated motion be described in terms of distance, velocity and time? (For our purpose this will involve plotting x & v as functions of t.)

2. How can we express the relationships among distance, velocity, time interval and acceleration in uniformly accelerated motion?

METHODOLOGICAL

Value Claims:
Completing the experiment and analysis of the experimental results will lead us to understand uniformly accelerated motion more fully and more meaningfully.

Knowledge Claims:
1. x vs. t graph for a uniformly accelerated motion with $V_0 = \theta$ is

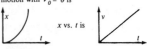

x vs. t is

2. The tangent of the curve x vs. t at a particular time t is equal to the v at the same time.
3. The area under the curve v vs. t up to a particular t is equal to the value for x at the same t.
4. Acceleration = the slope of v vs. t
= twice the slope of x vs. t^2
= ½ the slope of v^2 vs. x
5. g = _____cm/s^2 = the slope of a vs. θ.

Transformations:
Graphs of data

Records: for θ to 5 milliradian:
1. $\dfrac{\text{width of the card } \Delta x}{\text{the time for the card to pass the second gate}} = v$ at t $\dfrac{}{\Delta t}$

2. Plot x vs. t, v vs. t with θ fixed, find the tangent to the former curve and the area under the curve up to a particular value of t of the latter curve.

3. Plot x vs. t^2, v^2 vs. x, find the slope of each graph, also the slope of v vs. t. for $\theta = 10, 15$ milliradian:

4. Find a directly from the following equations instead of finding the slope
$a = v/t$, $a = v^2/2x$, $a = 2x/t^2$ for all θ's:

5. Plot a vs. θ find slope.

Event:
Moving a glider on an inclined air track with initial velocity equal to zero. (Digital timer and photocell gates are used for data recording.)

Figure 4.5 A Vee diagram showing the revised structure of a kinematics exercise in the laboratory guide for an introductory college physics course after it was modified to permit comprehension by the students (Chen 1980).

improvement in students' performance and in their attitude toward the laboratory exercise.[3]

Buchweitz (1981) used the Vee to analyze the laboratory guide for an advanced optics course and found a number of defects. He eval-

3   The physics course was taught in "mastery" mode (Bloom 1976), so Chen used the number of test trials needed to achieve passing (criterion) level as an index (average of 1.6 test trials for "new" version vs. 2.7 trials for "old"), and also had students complete an attitude questionnaire.

uated student performance on "concept ranking" tests, question-naires, and course exams and found that faulty learning occurred for those aspects of the laboratory work for which his Vee analysis showed deficiencies in the guide.

These are the two best examples we have at this time that demonstrate, by enhanced student achievement, that Vee diagrams can be a powerful tool for curriculum improvement. We are now completing work from other fields on subjects that may be more familiar to many readers than kinematics or optics.

5

NEW STRATEGIES
FOR EVALUATION:
CONCEPT MAPPING

TO MOST STUDENTS AND TEACHERS, achievement testing (usually true-false, multiple-choice, or short answer paper-and-pencil exams) is synonymous with evaluation of learning. Although this kind of evaluation will continue to have a role to play in the appraisal of learning, we believe a much wider range of practicable evaluation techniques are needed if we are to encourage students to use more of their human potential – evaluation, like other educative events, should help them recognize the great power they have to make sense out of events or objects experienced in their world.

While it is true that much testing has been of poor quality and that improving the traditional forms would contribute to the enhancement of learning, even the most well-designed objective tests correlate with subsequent achievement only in the range of $r = .2$ to $r = .7$. When we square these correlation coefficients to obtain the common variance shared by these measures we get values of only .04 to .49, so that at best only about 50 percent of variation in measures of achievement is predicted by any achievement measure or set of measures given within a few months to a year or two. The situation is unfortunately even worse: Subsequent achievement is usually measured by the same kind of testing used to measure current achievement; if other ways of assessing future success, for instance, the number of patents awarded to engineers, are used, then the correlation between school performance and achievement falls to near zero!

Hoffman's *Tyranny of Testing* (1962) cited many of the problems that derive from the widespread use of objective tests as virtually the only indicators of achievement. More recently, Gould has criticized testing practices in his book *The Mismeasure of Man* (1981). Unfortunately, practicable alternatives to objective testing have not been available. We believe that concept maps and Vee diagrams are two workable alternatives.

CONCEPT MAPPING AS AN EVALUATION TOOL

In the course of our research pursuing questions of how children acquire and use scientific concepts, we were constantly troubled by the fact that any variety of paper-and-pencil test we would devise did not validly measure the children's knowledge. By this we mean that if we sat down with children, one at a time, and asked them why they marked certain answers or what they meant when they chose their answers, we would often find that there was little correspondence between the content of the answers selected, as we interpreted the questions, and the meanings the children were expressing. To be sure, some of the difficulty was the limited ability of five-, six- or seven-year-old children to explain their answers. But even for the most articulate children, the same lack of correspondence existed between what we thought we were testing and what the children expressed as their understanding. There were exceptions, of course, and these become more frequent with older children. Even with college students, however, there is a surprising lack of correspondence between what the professor thinks is being tested and the actual meanings or thought processes the student is employing. In college physics, e.g., Gunstone & White (1981) and others have shown that though a student may be able to solve familiar problems and obtain correct answers on objective tests, other evaluation techniques (e.g., asking the student to attempt to solve a novel problem) may show that serious conceptual misunderstandings exist. The student has memorized an algorithm for getting the "right answer" but lacks an understanding of the concepts and propositions of physics that explain the phenomenon.

Initially our research questions were in the form, Can six-year-old children acquire a concept of energy? or Can seven-year-old children acquire an accurate concept of Earth and gravity? What became increasingly apparent was that the answers to these questions were never unequivocally yes or no, but rather "probably yes" for 10–20 percent of the children and "probably no" for another 10–20 percent. We became more conscious of the fact that the meaning a child acquires for any concept is evidenced not as all-or-none acquisition or failure to acquire, but rather as a growing set of propositional linkages between the concept of central concern and other related concepts. It was also evident that some students acquired faulty linkages and hence would say things like "Hard things are made of hard molecules and soft things are made of soft molecules," or "Things like water or air are made of water molecules (or air molecules)," but, when asked what was between the water molecules they would say "liquid water" or "just water." Without a concept of empty space, their "particulate models" for substances had serious defects. Our problem was to find reliable, consistent ways to express these varying degrees of concept understanding. We could not study the changes in or development of meanings of concepts in children over a span of years or as the result of instruction until we could devise a measurement tool that would recognize these changes in students' cognitive structures.

Richard Rowell (1978), working with tape recordings and transcripts of clinical interviews, decided to try to construct a "concept map template" and then to scan a given interview transcript to see if student responses to our interview questions indicated the presence of functional concepts and meaningful linkages between related concepts. Figure 5.1 shows an example of one of these maps, as well as a sample cognitive map constructed for one first-grade child in our sample. Notice that in these early maps we were not using linking words, hence the proposition formed by two concepts joined together had to be inferred. In various discussions, our colleague George Posner was very critical of the inherent ambiguity of our maps and this led us in time to construct concept maps as we described in Chapter 2. Our early work, stimulated in part by the good work in progress by Easley (1974) at the University of Illinois, convinced us that we were making progress in assessing changes in cognitive structure over a span of time (including analysis before and after instruction).

From 1974 through 1977, we began to use concept mapping as one of our evaluation tools in almost all of our research. We also began using concept maps with students in college biology and physics classes, both for evaluation of learning and as a learning aid for the students. During 1978–80, we conducted a research project teaching junior high school science students to construct concept maps and evaluating their performance in the use of maps (see Novak, Gowin, and Johansen 1983). The project was our primary impetus for writing this book, because it made it clear that students and teachers could use and benefit from our strategies.

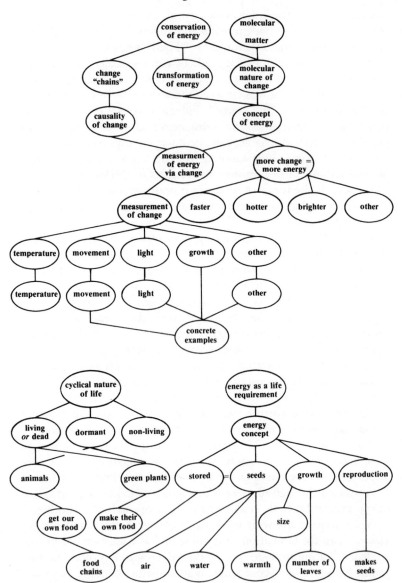

Figure 5.1 A concept map (top) prepared in 1973 to be used as a "template" to analyze interviews during our early work, and a sample student cognitive map (bottom) prepared for a first-grade child interviewed after instruction (Rowell 1978).

SCORING CONCEPT MAPS AS RELATED TO
LEARNING THEORY

Concept maps can be similar to paintings; you either like one or you do not. A simple qualitative judgment of students' concept maps is all that some teachers want. In our early work, we were often asked, "How does one score the children's concept maps?" We were more interested in representing what children's conceptual frameworks looked like before and after instruction, or over a span of years. Scoring was in many respects irrelevant, for we were looking for qualitative changes in the structure of children's concept maps. But because we live in a numbers-oriented society, most students and teachers want to score concept maps. So over the years we have devised a variety of scoring procedures, one of which was shown in Table 2.4.

The primary basis for our scoring schemes is Ausubel's cognitive learning theory, especially three ideas in it (look again at Figure 1.1): (1) Cognitive structure is *hierarchically organized,* with more inclusive, more general concepts and propositions superordinate to less inclusive, more specific concepts and propositions. (2) Concepts in cognitive structure undergo *progressive differentiation,* wherein greater inclusiveness and greater specificity of regularities in objects or events are discerned and more propositional linkages with other related concepts are recognized. and (3) *Integrative reconciliation* occurs when two or more concepts are recognized as relatable in new propositional meanings and/or when conflicting meanings of concepts are resolved. A full discussion of these ideas is beyond the scope of this book, but we can describe how these learning theory ideas can be translated into criteria for scoring concept maps.

Hierarchical structure. This idea incorporates Ausubel's concept of subsumption, namely that new information often is relatable to and subsumable under more general, more inclusive concepts. A good hierarchical structure for a segment of material to be learned begins with broad, inclusive concepts and then leads to more specific, less inclusive concepts. We have already noted that there can be no one "right" concept map; What we are striving to represent are good ways to see *hierarchies* of relationships, which are what concepts and concept maps are focused upon. Meanings, whether they are judged "right" or "wrong," are explicated in the relationships noted on concept maps. A concept map that seems to be upside down may signal either profound misunderstandings on the part of the student or an unusually creative way to look at concept relationships.

Hierarchy can also show the set of relationships between a concept and other concepts subordinate to it. In this way, hierarchy suggests differentiation of concepts in that it shows *specific* conceptual inter-relationships. The meaning we have for any given concept is dependent not only on the number of relevant relationships we perceive, but also on the hierarchy (inclusiveness) of those relationships in our conceptual frameworks. We are constantly seeking to observe, What concepts do we know that are relevant? and What higher-order– lower-order concept relationships are salient to this topic of study? These two questions are at the core of meaning of concept map hierarchies.

In order to construct a hierarchical concept map, one must think through what one perceives to be the most inclusive, less inclusive, and least inclusive concepts in any body of subject matter. This requires active cognitive thinking. In much school learning, it is easy for students to be relatively passive and to relate new knowledge to what they already know in an imprecise fashion. They may grasp the meaning of the new knowledge, but they have not meaningfully learned the new knowledge because they have not actively integrated it into their existing conceptual frameworks. Constructing a hierarchical concept map requires this kind of active integration of concepts.

An interesting way to observe the problems associated with integration of concept meanings is to ask students to save their first, second, and other intermediate concept maps and to turn these in together with their final map. Among the students we have worked with, we found two general patterns. Some students first develop smaller "submaps" combining 6 to 10 concepts and then integrate these into a larger final map. Other students begin by ranking the concepts to be mapped in some manner and then start constructing a map with 6 or 8 major concepts, gradually adding more subordinate concepts as they proceed. Either method can lead to well-organized, hierarchically structured concept maps. Without exception, students report that this work "really made them think," or helped them "to see relationships they never saw before."

Hierarchical structure also permits later subordination of a specific concept map into a more general, more inclusive map. As the study of a subject proceeds, the learner can grasp new relationships between topics that may before have appeared unrelated. To be able to link maps together during a course of study, students must grasp the meanings of new relationships between concepts in two or more subject areas.

Finally, hierarchical structure permits relatively easy assessment by the teacher, as sections of a concept map that are too general or too specific stand out and indicate either misunderstanding or the need for more careful integration of superordinate and subordinate concepts. One of the concept maps in Figure 5.2 illustrates these problems; the other, done by a student in the same fifth-grade class after hearing the same lecture, is by contrast remarkably well structured. It is important to recognize that creative students will see novel ways to represent concept relationships and hierarchies. The teacher must be alert to possible creative alternative hierarchies.

Progressive differentiation. Ausubel's principle of progressive differentiation states that meaningful learning is a continuous process wherein new concepts gain greater meaning as new relationships (propositional links) are acquired. Thus concepts are never "finally learned" but are always being learned, modified, and made more explicit and more inclusive as they become progressively more differentiated. Learning is the result of change in the meaning of experience, and concept maps are one method for showing both teacher and learner that real cognitive reorganization has occurred. For example, childrens' concept of weather, which at first may encompass little more than the difference between rain and sunshine, warm and cold, will in time take on much more precise meaning as it is linked to such concepts as solar radiation, the water cycle, and climatic patterns, and will continue to differentiate as they grow older if they attempt to learn more about the nature and causes of weather. Even meteorologists' concepts of weather will be further differentiated by their learning the results of new research.

Word association tests, in which subjects are given key concept words and then asked to list as many related words as they can in a fixed amount of time (say one minute), have also been used to measure concept development, but the difficulty with these tests is that they fail to indicate the propositional and hierarchical meanings of the related words.[1] Concept maps, on the other hand, because they represent specific propositional linkages (including hierarchical rela-

1 For a discussion of some of the issues here see Moreira 1977 and Stewart 1979.

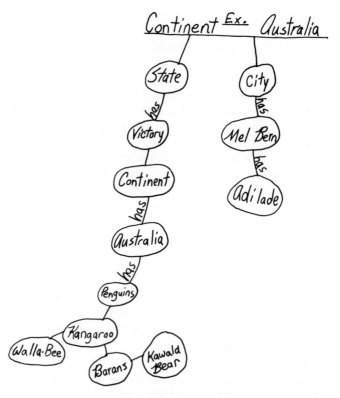

Figure 5.2 Concept maps prepared by two fifth-grade students after an illustrated slide lecture on Australia. One student's map (above) shows poor hierarchy with no clear distinction between general and specific concepts, whereas the other map (facing page) shows general and specific concepts in a remarkably good hierarchical structure.

tions) between concepts, are relatively precise indicators of the extent to which a person's concepts have been differentiated. Subjects must of course first be taught about concept maps and practice building them, but this drawback would be eliminated if all children were to learn to construct concept maps in the primary grades.

Most teachers know that it is important, before beginning instruction on a new topic, to have some idea of what their students already know (or misunderstand) about that topic. To put it in Ausubelian learning theory terms, a teacher needs to know what relevant con-

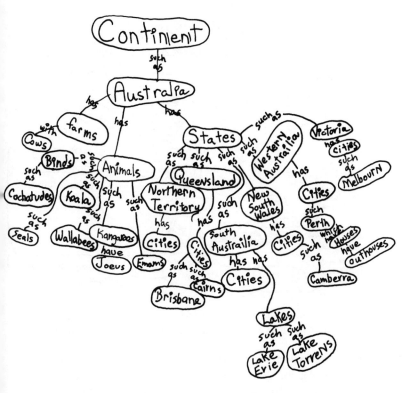

Figure 5.2 *(cont.)*

cepts can serve as the framework for subsumption of new material.
Concept maps are a simple tool for assessing where the learners are.

One approach is to select a key concept from the new topic for
study and to ask students to construct a concept map showing all the
concepts and relationships they can link to this key concept. In no
more than a quick glance over twenty or thirty concept maps, the
teacher can obtain a surprisingly good idea of how differentiated the
key concept already is for the students. Also, faulty linkages or misconceptions can be quickly spotted, and we know that these will
interfere with establishing desired new meanings unless specific steps
are taken to help students reorganize their concept maps.

Another way to assess the kind and extent of concept differentiation is to select 10 to 15 concepts from a new topic of study and ask
students to construct a concept map using these concepts. Figure 5.3

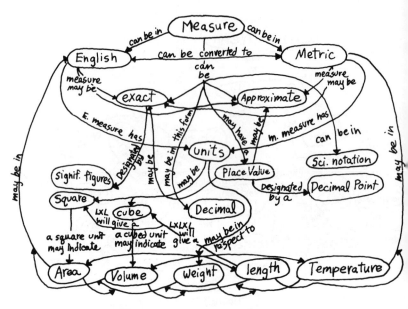

Figure 5.3 A good concept map prepared by a student as homework prior to discussion of a unit in a mathematics skills course (Minemier 1983).

shows an example of such a map constructed by a student in a math skills course. Again, a quick glance over these maps will show good or faulty linkages. In some cases, students will not have sufficient meaning for certain concept words to use them in their maps (students could be asked to circle or underline the concepts on the list that are unfamiliar). Students will sometimes use a concept that has a meaning for them that is not the meaning we wish to establish in the new instruction, which can help the teacher to alert students to the fact that the same label (word) familiar to them is being used to signify a new regularity (concept). Too often, teachers assume that students will recognize this fact, and students may go on attaching new concept meanings to the "wrong" concept without knowing why the subject matter appears to be inconsistent or confusing. As a result, they may resort to rote memorization and their misconceptions may go undetected and uncorrected.

Progressive differentiation of concepts is enhanced when concept maps for one topic are cross linked to concept maps for other, related topics. If specimen concept maps are posted around the classroom, students can be encouraged to see how the concept map for the current topic of study cross links to one or more concept maps for other topics. From time to time, a class discussion on ways to construct a higher order concept map to relate several topics of study can help to show the hierarchical relationships between concepts and the explanatory power of a few basic concepts. These activities help students progressively to differentiate their concepts and to gain both precision and inclusiveness in their concept meanings. Gifted students tend to do this reorganization on their own, but even they will profit from learning more systematic approaches to organizing knowledge, especially ways to see better its hierarchical structure. Less talented students usually resort to rote learning as the only alternative that allows them to maintain their self esteem in the face of an otherwise almost hopeless learning task. Less motivated students simply give up and become behavior problems or engage in what Holt (1964) called "strategies for failure."

A major source of sustained intrinsic motivation for learning is the positive emotional experience that derives from meaningful learning. Grades, awards, or reprisals provide extrinsic motivation for learning, and although they will continue to be used in school settings, we can do much to encourage a love for learning by helping students to find and recognize the good feelings that accompany the achievement of comprehensive meanings. Progressive differentiation of concepts through concept mapping can provide emotional as well as cognitive rewards, both in the short term and, especially, in the long term.

Integrative reconciliation. This principle of learning states that meaningful learning is enhanced when the learner recognizes new relationships (concept linkages) between related sets of concepts or propositions. For example, earlier in this chapter we discussed the common misconception that students see solids, liquids, or gases as made of "hard," or "watery" molecules. When students recognize that only empty space surrounds molecules and that the states of matter are related to temperature and the consequent molecular bonding patterns, they may integratively reconcile their old ideas with new ones: Ice or iron turn to liquid when heated not because the molecules have changed but because rigid bonds between molecules break up. And if more heat energy is added, the molecules may "fly apart" to form a gas that would expand indefinitely if it were not confined in a container. It may surprise some teachers and students to learn that metals can vaporize, but the dark coating inside an old lightbulb is condensed from vaporized tungsten from the hot filament.

Our example illustrates that meaningful learning requires a conscious awareness of new relationships between old and new sets of concepts. Furthermore, misconceptions must be consciously uncovered and displaced by new propositional linkages. Concept maps externalize the individual's propositional frameworks and can therefore be used to check on faulty linkages or to show what relevant concepts may be missing. Concept maps, used as tools for negotiating meaning, can make possible new integrative reconciliations that in turn lead to new and more powerful understanding.

Integrative reconciliation of concepts simultaneously results in at least some further differentiation of related concepts. When substantial alteration in concept meanings occurs (as in our example where the meanings of solid, liquid, and gas were radically altered), the resulting awareness of the new relationships produces the "ah ha!" feeling we get when we suddenly recognize a new meaning or relationship in a topic of study.

Concept maps that show valid cross links between sets of concepts that might otherwise be viewed as independent can suggest learners' integrative reconciliation of concepts. We can say only that cross links suggest integrative reconciliation, for it is possible for students to learn almost by rote that, for example, concept X in one cluster of concepts in a hierarchy is related to concept Z in another cluster of concepts in the conceptual framework. It is therefore often useful to probe beyond the meaning suggested by the linking words into how and why a given cross link is seen as important in order to separate glib linkages from substantive integrative reconciliation.

Creativity is often difficult to recognize, and even more difficult to illustrate to others. Substantial, novel integrative reconciliations are the major product of creative minds. To the extent that cross links can show novel concept integrations (at least to a student), such integrative reconciliations should be singled out and perhaps discussed with the class or given recognition in other positive ways. Creative ability is correlated with other abilities but is not the same. We find that some students who do poorly in regular classroom work demonstrate an exceptional ability in the nature and kind of cross links they may produce on their concept maps and the quality of the hierarchical structure of their maps. This kind of ability can be enormously important in real-world activities and needs to be given more recognition in school settings. Ricky, who produced the map shown in Figure 5.4, was an underachieving sixth grader (testing at about grade 4.5), but after a year of encouragement and motivation from having his good maps used for class discussions, he tested above his grade (at 7.6).

Scoring scales. We have tried a number of scoring schemes for concept maps over the years. The scoring key given in Table 2.4 is only one of these keys. Any scoring key for concept maps has a certain degree of subjectivity inherent in it, as in fact is the case with all evaluation instruments. True-false and multiple choice tests may score "objectively," but the choice of topics and the wording of questions are subjective and, to some extent, arbitrary. Essay or short-answer exams involve subjectivity in both the design of questions and the scoring of answers.

There is also an apparent arbitrariness in scoring concept maps: We specify that all maps should be hierarchical, all relationships should be labeled with appropriate linking words, and all cross links should be indicated. This apparent arbitrariness does not bias against any student or subject matter, unless research should show someday that some meaningful learning styles best demonstrate achievement with alternative concept map formats. To the extent that Ausubelian learning theory validly describes cognitive learning, and to the extent that our concept mapping procedures are consistent with these learning principles for achievement assessment, we believe the bias in our procedures is not deleterious. Concept maps may be said to have *construct validity* in terms of evaluation theory. There is a correspondence between assessment of cognitive performance and what our theory predicts should be the cognitive organization resulting from meaningful learning. Moreover, as we indicated earlier, we believe that concept maps have an epistemological as well as a psychological validity as tools for the assessment of learning (Novak, Gowin, and Johansen 1983).

The actual numerical value applied to each of the key scoring criteria is arbitrary, and we would encourage educators to experiment with different values. From our experience, the following are reasonable rules to follow in assigning numerical values (if such scoring is deemed necessary):

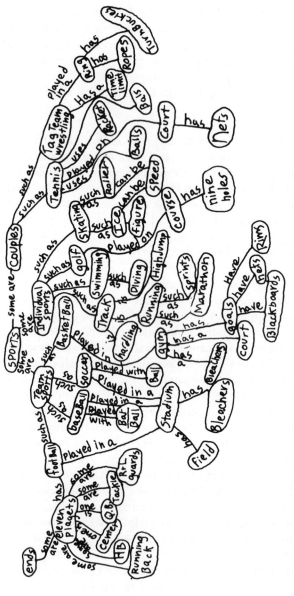

Figure 5.4 A concept map prepared by a sixth-grade student who was having trouble with schoolwork. This was the first concept map he prepared at home (with some revisions) after having been shown one example.

Evaluation strategies: concept mapping

(1) Score all relationships that are valid (form valid propositions). You may wish to subtract wrong or ambiguous concept linkages, but this may complicate scoring unnecessarily. Valid cross-link relationships might be scored also, or simply weighted into rule 3 below.

(2) Count valid levels of hierarchy and score each level X times as much as each relationship. The value for X is arbitrary, but because maps have many more relationships than hierarchies, and because valid hierarchies signal progressive differentiation and integrative reconciliation of concept meanings, it seems reasonable and valid to score each level of the hierarchy 3 to 10 times as much as each relationship. Scoring levels of hierarchy when maps are not symmetrical is a problem, but we suggest that the number of valid hierarchies in the most branched segment of the map be counted. Words that have simply been strung together without clear subordinate conceptual relationships, however, should not count as levels of hierarchies (see Figure 5.5).

(3) Cross links that show valid relationships between two distinct segments of the concept hierarchy signal possibly important integrative reconciliations, and may therefore be better indicators of meaningful learning than are hierarchical levels. We suggest that each valid cross link receive 2 or 3 times the points assigned to each hierarchical level. Since it is possible to construct some kind of cross link between almost any two concepts on a map, you must use judgment to decide if a given cross link represents substantial integrative reconciliation of two sets of concepts. As with essay exams, students may want to defend their answers, and you can expect some negotiation with them on this aspect of scoring. If you view concept mapping primarily as a learning tool, these negotiations might be as valuable to the student as the map construction.

(4) It may be desirable to ask for specific examples in some cases to be sure that the students know what kind of event or object is designated by the concept label. You may want to score valid examples the same as relationships, or perhaps give them half as many points because they are usually easy to supply and less indicative of meaningful learning. It is possible for students to rote learn that a cat is an example of the concept mammal (or that ice is an example of a solid) without knowing the regularity the concept designates. Of course, because concept links can be learned by rote as well, not all relationships will signal meaningful learning.

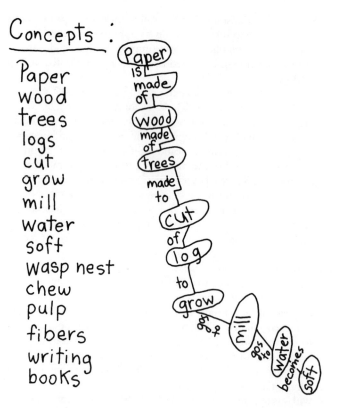

Figure 5.5 A concept map made by a fourth-grade student showing a linear string of words without clear subordinate conceptual relationships. Such strings should not count as levels of hierarchies. This student was the best oral reader in her class, but showed little comprehension of what she read. Her map suggests a rote, verbatim approach to reading, which does not lead to acquisition of meaning.

We believe that these scoring criteria, when applied with an understanding of meaningful learning principles, can assess learning at least as effectively as most other evaluation approaches. Readers should experiment with their own scoring keys and refinements of scoring criteria. One of the purposes of this book is to encourage such experimentation, and we hope we will later be able to share experiences with others.

6

THE USE OF THE VEE
FOR EVALUATION

VALUE AND EVALUATION:
WHAT HAS EDUCATIONAL VALUE?

IT SHOULD BE OBVIOUS that evaluation rests on the judgment of value. To evaluate, we must have a clear notion of value. Is this piece of knowledge or segment of curriculum valuable? Do this student's claims about this article, this poem, this laboratory, or this piece of mathematics have value? The Vee heuristic is useful for answering these kinds of value questions. Refer again to Figures 1.2 and 3.1 showing the elements of the Vee that, when considered together, function in a normative way to set the criteria of value. A good piece of knowledge should embody all elements of the Vee, illustrate how those elements are connected to each other, and be coherent, comprehensive, and meaningful.

Teachers often struggle with the question, Is this a good lesson? or Is this a good answer to my question? As a normative tool, the Vee tells us that a good lesson, or good answer, should make clear what segment of the world we are dealing with – the events or objects that are of concern – and should show how the other elements of the Vee function integratively to make sense of observations regarding these events or objects. If elements of the Vee are missing or not clear – key concepts or principles omitted; records not clearly linked to the events or objects they describe; principles, theory, or philosophy not stated or implied; claims ambiguously linked to records, principles, and so on – then we can judge that the lesson or answer is faulty. The question, Does the lesson (or student answer) cover the ground? can be answered more easily when we ask, Does the lesson (or student answer) cover the elements of the Vee? This, then, becomes the criterion of value, of educational worth.

To evaluate should require us to have a clear notion of value. Unfortunately, the professional practice of evaluation seldom worries about value. The standard devices (achievement tests, for example) tell us almost nothing about what is worth knowing and how we are to judge the worth of knowledge. In our view, the educational value of any "object" (lecture, text, lab manual, experiment, book, test, educational event) resides in how well it can help us to realize our power to understand the world we inhabit: It should transform the meaning of our experience so that both we and our world have enriched meaning. Concept maps and Vee diagrams help us to think better by organizing meaning in a more coherent and comprehensive way. Thinking based on understanding leads to actions that are better controlled (more efficient, more effective). And being able to act with such confidence makes us feel better about ourselves and our world.

The very possibility of educational worth, like the possibility of educating itself, rests upon the fact that meanings can be shared. Meanings are social constructions that allow us on the one hand to exercise the powers of inference, self-understanding, and thoughtful action and on the other, to tie things together and connect part to part to whole. Our concern with grasping meaning, reorganizing meaning through meaningful learning, and sharing meaning in interactions of teachers and students is summed up in the definition of governance: Controlling meaning controls effort. Good educative experiences should help us control meaning so that it leads to desirable human effort and satisfaction.

To understand educational value, we must have a theory of educating that tells us what clearly does and does not count as educating. But educational evaluation has not so far been guided by theory. Book after book on educational evaluation fail us because they fail to specify what constitutes an instance of teaching or learning, or of curriculum or governance. There are handbooks published on teacher evaluation that never face the conceptual task of defining what we mean by "teaching." Definitions of the key concepts in educating would tell us what any event – "teaching," for example – is to mean. Making clear what we mean is important because when we control meaning we control effort. To give answers to a typical, topical evaluation question like, Is science teaching worse in 1983 than in 1973? we must first decide what we mean by "science teaching" – and that is a task of concept analysis. Neither factual nor valuational claims about science teaching will help us decide what to do to change practice if we do not have a working concept of "science teaching." A thoughtfully constructed concept map that tied together the various aspects of "science teaching" would be of direct help.

Consider again this last paragraph. We are touting the value of our heuristics. But the merits or demerits of heuristics like these cannot be read off the surface of the page. They were not designed to mirror their domain or to contain unassailable internal logic (cf., Rorty, *Philosophy and the Mirror of Nature,* 1979). Rather, the merit of these heuristics is found only as they are used. Do they guide actions? Do they demystify knowledge making? Do they help students and teachers come into possession of meaning, and hence power? In other words, when one takes these ideas and uses them, what happens? The answer to that question is the authority upon which those views rest.

USING VEE DIAGRAMS

Vee diagrams help to organize thinking, to make actions (in the laboratory, for instance) more efficient and productive, and to make students feel better about themselves because they understand what they are doing. Educational value is enhanced by students' integration of thinking, feeling, and acting. That educational evaluation concerns the value of education is a point often misunderstood in standard methods of testing, measuring, and evaluating, which seek to elicit information from students that exactly mirrors a text or lesson. Our heuristic, on the other hand, asks students to reorganize new information using what they already know, a process that is creative and idiosyncratic and that requires that understanding be expressed through a variety of ways of thinking and doing. Educational value is determined by what the learners *do* with lessons, not by the exact fit between a lesson and its replication on a test. Educational value is a transformation of the quality of experience that empowers students to give meaning to themselves and to their world, and the value of education can only be judged by its power to bring about educational consequences.

As we noted earlier, the Vee shape of the heuristic device is to some extent arbitrary (it could also be ladder shaped, or a line continuum with the events and objects at the center). We have continued to find symbolic and representational value in the Vee form. Our major vacillations have been over how to represent the crucially important interplay between the conceptual-thinking-theoretical elements on the left side and the procedural-doing-methodological elements on the right side. It is crucially important that students recognize this interplay, or interaction, between "thinking" and "doing" in any field of human endeavor where we seek to create new knowledge. The two sides of the Vee are obviously interdependent; what is not so obvious is the inextricable necessity for recognizing that concepts, principles, and theories influence what we see in and do with observations, and that these observations in turn gradually influence the concepts, principles, and theories we construct. The problem is where to begin our analysis of knowledge construction, for there is no way to decide what comes first or what is most important. Both thinking and doing activities are important when we endeavor to create new knowledge, and these activities are significantly influenced by the events or objects we choose to observe.

We believe that educational evaluation can be improved if we take cognizance of our understanding of how humans create and appraise knowledge and the psychological processes by which they come to understand knowledge. None of the published books on educational evaluation explicitly considers these ideas, and this has been a major shortcoming in educational measurement theory and practice based on the early work of Binet and others since the turn of the century. We believe that we may be on the threshold of a new era in the assessment of human potential and achievement, not because better IQ tests or achievement tests may be devised, but rather because we are developing a new conceptual framework through which to view the nature and problems of assessment of human aptitudes and abilities. We hope that this book will stimulate such activity.

THE VEE AS A TOOL FOR EVALUATION
IN PRACTICAL SETTINGS

For laboratory, studio, or field work, the Vee can serve as an especially valuable evaluation tool. The fundamental question in these settings is always, What do these things we are observing mean? What is special or significant about these events and/or objects? Our contention has been that the significance of any event or object is dependent upon the concepts and principles through which it is viewed. An experiment, poem, painting, or building has only the richness or quality that our ideational constructs allow us to see. This reciprocal relationship between what we see and our interpretations is the basis of human understanding and obviously has important implications for evaluation.

The simplest way to use the Vee for evaluation is to ask the students to "lay the Vee" on claims about events or objects and then to describe each of the elements of the Vee as they interpret them, using the ten questions given in the section on reading material in Chapter 3. This requires that students penetrate far deeper than the relatively disconnected facts or details in an inquiry, or experiment, or than the more trivial information in an exposition or report in which claims are being made about any subject. Though it is usually not possible for students to gain the information needed to answer all of the questions, this systematic search for answers requires the best thinking they are capable of, and rewards them by helping them realize both that constructing knowledge is a complex activity and that they can learn to master the process.

It should be evident that "laying the Vee" on claims about events or objects is a task rarely possible from rote memory. It requires not only interpretation, but also analysis, synthesis, and evaluation of knowledge – the highest levels of Bloom's (1956) taxonomy of educational objectives. In spite of the relatively challenging nature of Vee making, our experience has been that students react positively to this task. Especially when compared with more traditional written reports, Vee making is a shorthand approach to exposing students' understanding of a topic or area of study and also helps them to organize ideas and information. Students recognize that Vee making, besides being less tedious than writing reports, helps them to gain understanding of the subject matter. Vee making also gives students the positive feelings that come with the perception of increased meaningfulness. When students feel better about their accomplishments, they are more willing to work, and they are more likely to take responsibility for their own learning.

USING THE VEE TO ASSESS STUDENTS' UNDERSTANDING OF EXPOSITORY MATERIALS

Students need practice and assistance in writing expository material; Vee making is not a substitute for this work but an alternative that can be employed profitably, especially for reporting on an inquiry. Furthermore, Vee making can be followed on occasion by oral or written expositions, and the results are likely to be more communicative than reports not preceded by Vee analysis. We find that setting aside a few minutes to diagram an exposition can be faster than conventional outlining or rough drafts. Our graduate students and colleagues who have used the strategy have found that whatever the form of the final exposition, Vee mapping can be a useful and time-saving intermediate step.

Student use of Vees is important in evaluation. In one study in school biology classes, the teacher required students to draw Vee diagrams before entering the laboratory (Gurley 1982; see Figure 8.4). Students so instructed spent more than 90 percent of their time in the laboratory on task-related activities, whereas students not so instructed did only half as well (only 40 percent of their time was spent on content or task-related activities). Moreover, Vee diagrams help students to organize their thinking, to make their actions more efficient and productive, and, what we think is extremely important, to feel better about themselves and take more responsibility for what they are doing.

THINKING AND DOING

Figure 6.1 shows the construction for a high school biology teacher of a Vee with the left side labeled "thinking" and the right side labeled "doing." As a general orientation this works well, especially because it emphasizes that one must first think carefully about experimental work before carrying it out. Karl Marx wrote that the important difference between the very best bee and the very worst architect is that the latter first constructs in imagination what a structure is to be like. And so it is; thinking is a form of imagining, of creating structures of meaning, remaking them, and, in effect, redoing them. The point being that thinking is also doing. We do something when we are thinking. We push ideas and meanings around. We change our minds. A series of rapidly composed concept maps shows almost literally this process of thinking, of pushing concepts around, of redoing the meanings of things. Thinking as a human activity is related to but different from doing, wherein objects are constructed and pushed about (as in a laboratory), made and remade (as in an artist's studio). The objective, educationally speaking, is not merely to understand but to make better, not merely to grasp meaning but to reorganize other meanings so that insight occurs, not merely to learn lessons but to live better. And to do this requires us to take an

The use of the Vee for evaluation

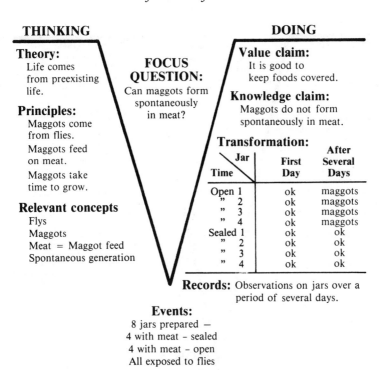

THINKING

DOING

Theory:
Life comes
from preexisting
life.

Principles:
Maggots come
from flies.
Maggots feed
on meat.
Maggots take
time to grow.

Relevant concepts
Flys
Maggots
Meat = Maggot feed
Spontaneous generation

**FOCUS
QUESTION:**
Can maggots form
spontaneously
in meat?

Value claim:
It is good to
keep foods covered.

Knowledge claim:
Maggots do not form
spontaneously in meat.

Transformation:

Jar Time	First Day	After Several Days
Open 1	ok	maggots
" 2	ok	maggots
" 3	ok	maggots
" 4	ok	maggots
Sealed 1	ok	ok
" 2	ok	ok
" 3	ok	ok
" 4	ok	ok

Records: Observations on jars over a
period of several days.

Events:
8 jars prepared —
4 with meat – sealed
4 with meat – open
All exposed to flies

Figure 6.1 A Vee diagram prepared from the description of an experiment
in a high school biology textbook. This kind of analysis helps students to
focus carefully on relevant details of an experiment.

action in the world. Such action-taking requires doing, but doing
that is fueled by thinking. As thinking is one kind of doing, doing
also requires thinking. We do not want to separate the arms of the
Vee by a simple-minded dichotomy between thinking and doing.
We want to be able to see just how they are both involved in our
getting smart about ourselves and our world.

Vee mapping can help students to organize written or oral exposition, and it can also be used as a tool for evaluating students' understanding of exposition. As we noted in Chapter 3, we have found
almost all written research reports to contain flaws, often serious
ones, in meaning or conclusions when they are analyzed with the
Vee heuristic. Even papers that appear to be clear and well reasoned
will often show ambiguities or faulty conclusions. Ten questions that

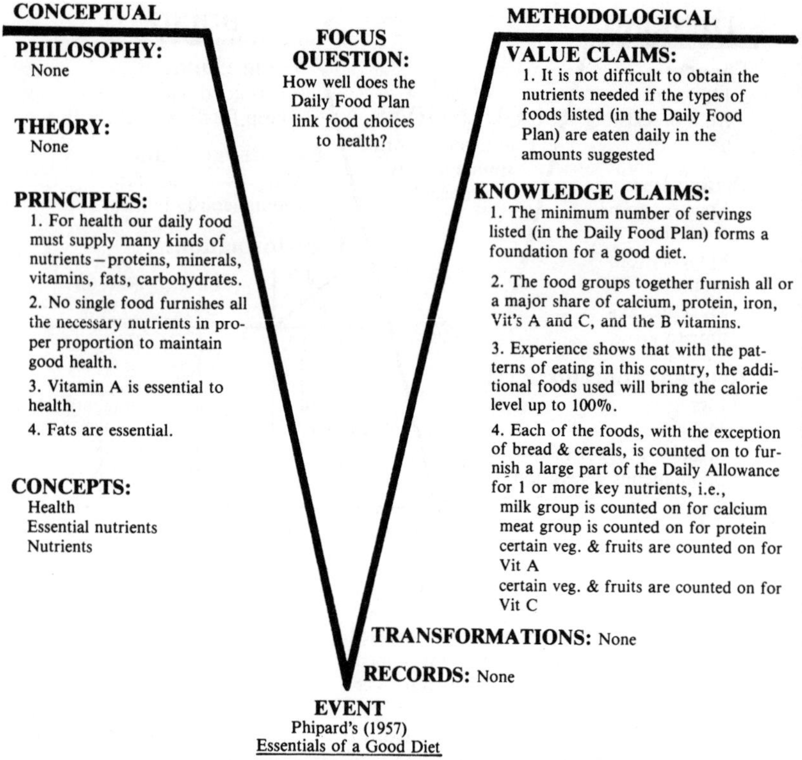

CONCEPTUAL

PHILOSOPHY:
None

THEORY:
None

PRINCIPLES:
1. For health our daily food must supply many kinds of nutrients – proteins, minerals, vitamins, fats, carbohydrates.

2. No single food furnishes all the necessary nutrients in proper proportion to maintain good health.

3. Vitamin A is essential to health.

4. Fats are essential.

CONCEPTS:
Health
Essential nutrients
Nutrients

FOCUS QUESTION:
How well does the Daily Food Plan link food choices to health?

METHODOLOGICAL

VALUE CLAIMS:
1. It is not difficult to obtain the nutrients needed if the types of foods listed (in the Daily Food Plan) are eaten daily in the amounts suggested

KNOWLEDGE CLAIMS:
1. The minimum number of servings listed (in the Daily Food Plan) forms a foundation for a good diet.

2. The food groups together furnish all or a major share of calcium, protein, iron, Vit's A and C, and the B vitamins.

3. Experience shows that with the patterns of eating in this country, the additional foods used will bring the calorie level up to 100%.

4. Each of the foods, with the exception of bread & cereals, is counted on to furnish a large part of the Daily Allowance for 1 or more key nutrients, i.e.,
milk group is counted on for calcium
meat group is counted on for protein
certain veg. & fruits are counted on for Vit A
certain veg. & fruits are counted on for Vit C

TRANSFORMATIONS: None

RECORDS: None

EVENT
Phipard's (1957)
Essentials of a Good Diet

Figure 6.2 A Vee diagram prepared from a published report (Page and Phipard 1957) dealing with nutrition (Cheryl Achterberg, personal communication).

can be used in this kind of analysis were presented in the section on reading material in Chapter 3.

In our work with secondary school and college students, we have found the Vee to be applicable to textbook or other expository materials. Figure 6.1 shows a textbook experiment mapped onto a Vee. Text material other than experiments can also be mapped, as is shown in Figure 6.2. Some text materials do not lend themselves to Vee making and might be best scrutinized through concept mapping. This is particularly true of descriptive material that does not involve knowledge claims based on data of some kind.

We have also noted that Vee diagramming is a useful tool for analysis of material for purposes of curriculum development. Curriculum making is a complex and difficult endeavor calling for the best minds in their brightest hours. (For a careful exposition of what is required see Novak 1977, chapters 5 and 6, and Gowin 1981, chapter 4.) Papers, texts, literary works, lectures, and other forms of exposition can be analyzed and critically evaluated using the Vee. Our students have applied Vee analysis to curriculum materials in virtually every field, and have found them often to be seriously deficient in key elements necessary to acquire understanding of the material.

THEORY-LADEN OBSERVATION

A large number of philosophers of science (e.g., Kuhn 1962) have accepted the view that all scientific observation is theory laden. They have used this view to deny the view of early logical positivism, which claimed that all scientists must give up their theories when the facts (observations) do not support them. Any theory in conflict with experimental or observational evidence must be abandoned, claimed the young positivists in their zeal to discredit the nonfactual authority of the church, of idealistic metaphysics, or of irrational political power (Nazism). But the view that observations are laden with theoretical meaning is only partly correct; it is partly just confused, and partly wrong.

The Vee diagram, and its definitions of concept and fact, show us how to avoid this confusion. The easiest way to make the distinction is to claim that concept and fact are different elements in the structure of knowledge. In any new case of constructing knowledge, we must integrate the concepts with regularities in events and with records of these events. That snug integration at the bottom of the Vee gives validity to upper layers of the structure of knowledge. A complication occurs when we realize that we do have "theories of the instrument," that is, the robust conceptualizations in science of how to measure things, how to observe them, how to make records of them (interests on the right side). Through records, we can make facts that are repeatable, reliable, and consistent but have no meaning, or rather, what they mean awaits another theory – "the theory of the event." Factor analysis in educational research is a case in point: After orthogonal rotation has let the factors drop out, there is still the need to say what the factors mean. As John Dewey wrote often, there is nothing on the face of a fact that tells us what it means. We need theories, ideas, conceptual structures, imagination, world views, and so on, for that special office in human understanding. In each case we must decide the relative weighting of the theory of the instrument versus the theory of the event.

Vee diagrams represent a student's attempt to express how some segment of knowledge is constructed. The scoring suggestions offered in Table 3.3 were constructed with a view both to providing a practicable scheme for busy teachers and to encompassing certain epistemological principles. As one gains experience with Vees, readings in philosophy dealing with the nature of knowledge take on much increased meaning. Conversely, some of these readings will provide new insights into interpreting students' answers, greater comprehension of the elements of the Vee, and a growing confidence as to how and why the use of a heuristic of this type is valuable. It would not be surprising to find at least an occasional student who becomes interested in a career as an epistemologist as a result of this kind of teaching. With millions of persons involved in the production and transmission of knowledge, the world could benefit from more work by inspired epistemologists.

7

THE INTERVIEW AS AN EVALUATION TOOL

THE ORIGINS of the interview go back to the nineteenth-century work of psychoanalysts, although forms of systematic questioning were used in early Greek and Roman times, or before. It was largely Jean Piaget and his colleagues in Switzerland, however, who perfected the interview as a tool for assessing cognitive capabilities in the 1920s and 1930s, and it is to Piaget and his coworkers that we owe the development of interview strategies for use with children.

Piaget's approach was to present very carefully selected specific objects or events to children and to ask carefully worded specific questions. As the tasks and questions were developed over time, Piaget found that the responses of children in selected age ranges could be characterized into a small set of groups, or *stages*. The relatively high degree of predictability of children's responses in these interviews provided support for Piaget's theory of cognitive development, which was widely used in the United States in the 1960s and 1970s to explain why students failed at certain learning tasks.

Piaget's theory, and associated interview methods for making records of children's reasoning, led to the observation of four stages of development: (1) sensory motor (prereasoning responses, ages 0 to 2), (2) preoperational responses (interpretations of tangible objects or events on the basis of manifest attributes as perceived by the child, ages 2 to 7), (3) concrete operational responses (responses based on reasoning, but only about manifest attributes, ages 7 to 14), and (4) formal reasoning responses ("abstract" thinking about objects or events, ages 14 and above). Part of Piaget's genius was in devising the specific interview events and objects and the questions that made it possible to observe regularities in children's responses (i.e., their claims about the events or objects). From these observed regularities, Piaget constructed concepts, principles, and a theory of cognitive development. He demonstrated what we see relatively rarely in the sciences: the genius needed to create new methodologies, concepts, principles, and theory to explain a naturally occurring phenomenon.

Behavioral psychologists harshly criticized Piaget's work, since a key tenet of their own philosophy was that we should not speculate on the inner workings of the mind (reasoning patterns) but only on manifest behavior. Because behaviorism was the dominant psychology in the United States, Piaget's work received little attention until behaviorism began to decline and his work was "rediscovered" in the 1960s (Ripple and Rockcastle 1964). More recently, however, there has been renewed criticism of Piaget's ideas on the grounds that his theory too severely constrained his interview methods and led to too narrow interpretations of the interview records (see, for example, Novak 1977b, Donaldson 1978, Modgil and Modgil 1982, and Macnamara 1982). What Piaget failed to recognize adequately is the powerful role language development and specific frameworks of relevant concepts play in the development of children's patterns of reasoning. The half century of work done by Piaget and his coworkers is, nevertheless, monumental, and there remains much in his thinking about the relationship between children's experiences with objects and events in the world and their cognitive development that has value. We shall always be indebted to Piaget for his popularization of the interview method.

PLANNING AN INTERVIEW

In the terminology of the Vee, interview tasks are events we construct with students,[1] and the records we obtain will be dependent upon the task we set and the questions we ask. The interview format can vary from highly flexible (with both tasks and questions varying from student to student) to highly standardized (with carefully specified tasks and questioning patterns). Piagetian interviews fall into the latter category. Tasks and/or questions can range narrowly or broadly, and the records that result from different approaches are

---

1 We will use the term "students" to refer to the individuals interviewed rather than the term "subject" or "S" commonly used in psychology: In most causes, the "subjects" will indeed be students, and this will also avoid confusion between the content or subject matter of the interview and the interviewee.

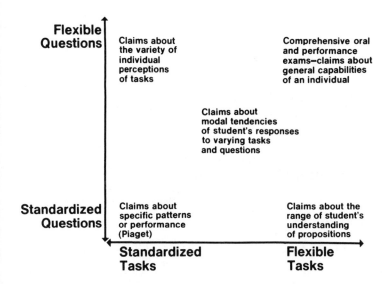

Figure 7.1 Types of knowledge claims that can be made from interviews, represented on task and question format continua. Different theoretical interests will favor different degrees of task and/or question flexibility.

useful for different purposes (for making different sets of knowledge claims). Figure 7.1 illustrates the task and question continuums and the kinds of knowledge claims that can be generated from the records obtained. Of course, we could choose our tasks almost at random and ask subjects any question that comes to mind, but although we may have a lively, interesting dialog with a student, we may have great difficulty persuading others as to that student's specific knowledge or abilities. Ironically, the "best" oral exams for graduate degrees (albeit successful only with very able students) are those in which highly idiosyncratic questioning covers a broad range of topics, although such questioning serves to reveal the general status of a student's knowledge rather than knowledge of a specific area.

There are several reasons for choosing interview tasks and questions with varying degrees of flexibility. It should be kept in mind, however, that we are trying to look into the student's cognitive structure and ascertain not only what concepts and propositions are there, but also how those concepts are structured and how they can be evoked for problem solving. A narrow spectrum of tasks and/or

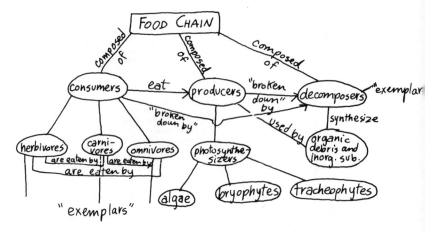

Figure 7.2 A concept map prepared to plan student interviews on the food chain.

questions may therefore fail to reveal knowledge or abilities that are highly relevant to a broader assessment of abilities.

Selecting content. Interviews can be developed for any subject matter. Although it is possible to design interviews to assess students' attitudes and values, we will not deal with this area; other works are available that provide some guidance in this area (Gilligan 1982, for example). Our concern is with the students' individual frameworks of knowledge and reasoning strategies. In Chapter 2, we quoted Ausubel's dictum that "the most important single factor influencing learning is what the learner already knows" (Ausubel 1968, epigraph). Our principal objective in an interview is to ascertain what the learner knows about a given body of knowledge. Prior to instruction, the interview will help in the selection and organization of concepts and examples. After instruction, interviews can help educators assess the degree to which they have been successful in achieving shared meanings with the students.

The length of an interview depends partly on the age of the children involved and partly on the purpose of the interview, but in no case should it last more than 15 to 30 minutes. In this time frame, we can only expect to probe a small segment of a student's knowledge or reasoning patterns, but interviews work best when they deal with

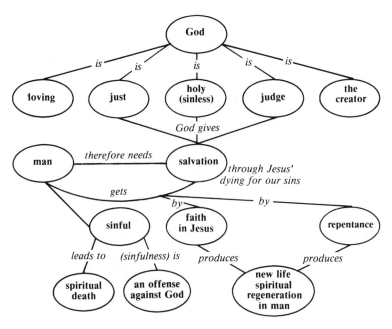

Figure 7.3 A concept map prepared to plan an interview with adults on their concepts of spiritual salvation.

a closely related set of concepts and propositions and their application in the tasks presented. A good way to plan an interview is to prepare a concept map for a segment of subject matter so as to identify key concepts and propositions. Figure 7.2 shows a concept map prepared in planning an interview on food chains, and Figure 7.3 is a map used to plan an interview with adults on their ideas about spiritual salvation.

The concepts and propositions in our concept map can guide us in selecting auxiliary materials or tasks for the interview and in structuring our questions. Many of our early interviews were planned in this way and then refined and revised through experience with students. In our more recent work, however, we have employed a different strategy, which we have found to be more efficient: After identifying key concepts in a subject area of interest to us, we ask a sample of students to construct concept maps using all or some of these key concepts and encourage them to add other concepts they

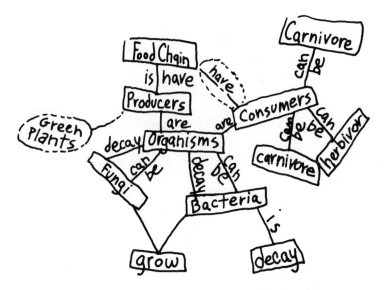

Figure 7.4 A concept map prepared by a student that shows faulty propositions (e.g., bacteria is decay) or missing key concepts (added in dotted ovals) such as green plants.

deem relevant. (The term *sample* recognizes that we are always dealing with a segment of a larger group – the *population* of all persons who share attitudes similar to our sample.) From twenty or thiry concept maps prepared by a group (perhaps one class in the middle of the age range of interest to us), we can quite easily identify a large number of valid propositions, and many misconceptions, or invalid propositions as well. All of this may be accomplished in only a few hours' time, even if it is first necessary to instruct the sample group in making concept maps. (If the students are beginners at concept mapping, some of their misconceptions may simply represent a lack of mapping skill, but most will be valid misconceptions that are present in at least some of the selected population.) Before we began using these student concept maps, we often found it necessary to construct, administer, evaluate, and revise interviews five or six times before we began to see consistent patterns of answers, a process that took anywhere from 30 to 100 hours. Even for a research worker, there are limits to how much time can be devoted to developing a

Table 7.1. *Faulty propositions from students' concept maps on the food chain*

1. Food chains are producers
2. Producers are consumers
3. Producers may be animals
4. Producers are carnivores
5. Consumers can be producers
6. A consumer is a decomposer
7. Consumers "have" carnivores
8. Bacteria is decay
9. An omnivore could not eat plants
10. Producers can be organisms
11. A horse is a carnivore
12. Carnivores eat grass
13. Omnivores can eat plants (animals not included)
14. Organisms are producers (consumers not included)
15. Some decomposers are organisms
16. Omnivores not linked with food
17. Producers, consumers, and decomposers not distinguished in food chain

suitable interview, and for teachers these time requirements are pro-hibitive. Using student concept mapping as a starting point, good interviews can be constructed in 1 to 5 hours with only one or two revisions.

Figure 7.4 shows a fourth-grade student's concept map with invalid or missing concepts. Shown in Table 7.1 are 17 other faulty or invalid propositions gleaned from thirty concept maps prepared by this class. For each of the faulty propositions, it is relatively easy to construct questions that would probe each student's cognitive structure to ascertain whether or not misconceptions exist and if so, how they are related to other ideas held in the student's mind.

Structuring questions. The concept maps prepared by the sample group also serve as the primary source for questions to be incorporated into the interview. For example, the following questions are suggested by the faulty propositions listed in Table 7.1:

(1) Is every plant and animal a producer? (from proposition 1)
(2) Are all consumers decomposers ? (from proposition 6)

(3) Are there any plants that ominivores eat? Do horses eat meat as well as plants? (from proposition 9)

(4) Do ominivores need food? (from proposition 16)

Selecting auxiliary materials. To sustain a student's interest throughout an interview, it is necessary to provide props, activities, or demonstrations from which one may then proceed with questions that probe the student's understanding. These auxiliary materials can be crucially important: The ultimate power and validity of an interview may rest on how successfully they have been chosen and constructed.

The first step is to review the questions generated from the concept maps and consider what props, activities, or demonstrations would serve as visual or tactile references. Pictures or drawings, which are relatively easy to locate or prepare, are often useful. Or sets of pictures can be used, and the student asked to arrange them in some order. For example, pictures of the sun, grass, a rabbit, a fox, and so on, could be presented for the food chain example, and the student asked to arrange them and then explain why the sun was put first, grass next, and so on. Additional questions might be interposed to clarify the reasoning behind the student's choices. Collages of pictures can be very useful also. Models or mock-ups showing events and/or objects relevant to the concepts of interest can be the basis for good questions such as, What is going on here? or, Can you explain how this works? Such models must be accurate and chosen with care. We are interested in having the student reveal as many of the concepts and propositions in his or her existing cognitive structure as is possible in a short time, and poorly chosen models may be counterproductive because they can lead to digressions from the subject matter or introduce new confusion.

Textbooks, teachers' guides, and reference works can be good sources of ideas for auxiliary materials. In most cases, however, activities or demonstrations will have to be modified; the questions generated from the concept maps, together with a trial interview, will usually provide the necessary guidance. Including too many activities in one interview can lead to confusion; four or five tasks are usually optimal for one interview session.

Trial interviews can be conducted with as few as three students representative of a population, and most of the major problems with an interview will usually be revealed with a sample of five or six students. For interviews that are especially difficult to develop, it is more efficient to use only a few students in a tryout, revise, and then test the revisions. A "perfect" interview is not a realistic goal, for even interviews developed over years and used with hundreds of students still reveal less than a perfect picture of students' knowledge and thinking strategies. Human cognitive structures are so idiosyncratic that no one interview can reveal with perfect fidelity the cognitive frameworks of all students. Interviews developed with the strategies we suggest can, however, provide an enormous amount of valid data on what students know and how they use this knowledge.

Sequencing questions. If an interview is constructed from student concept maps, it is easy to devise many good questions. What is not so easy is to determine the sequence of questions. Because almost all concepts are related in some way in cognitive structure, it might seem that we could use any concept or relationship to begin probing a student's understanding. Such an arbitrary start is not feasible, however, for several reasons. First, if students experience difficulty with the beginning question(s), they may become nervous and "clutch up," thus inhibiting their responses to other questions. Second, if the first questions are too easy or the answers too obvious, students may "turn off" and not try to give you their best performance. Third, for questions to flow smoothly, it is important that the first question lead easily to the second, and so on.

The best beginning questions are open-ended ones that cannot be answered by yes or no or a simple statement of fact. Questions like When did the American Revolution begin? or Are presidents in the United States elected directly by the people? would be poor opening questions. Much better would be, What did the British tea tax have to do with the American Revolution? or Why is it important for a U.S. presidential candidate, in order to be successful, to win small majorities in many states rather than very large majorities in a few states?

Good auxiliary materials serve as the best starting points for questioning. Open-ended questions such as How would you explain what is happening here? or What can you tell me about this (picture, model, or demonstration)? will usually elicit a train of comments from which other questions (many of them suggested by the concept maps) can easily follow.

As a general rule, it is best to proceed from more to less familiar areas of subject matter and from broad to detailed questions. This sequence helps interviewees to collect their thoughts so that they reveal more about what they know. Because an interview usually underestimates the knowledge a student has about a topic, we always strive to probe into cognitive structure as extensively as is practicable. If we probe enough, we can almost always find misconceptions or apparent gaps in knowledge that may lead to subsequent difficulties in learning. Ferreting out all the relevant elements of cognitive structure is difficult; most evaluation procedures tap only a portion. The clinical interview, when well executed, provides by far the most penetrating assessment of a student's knowledge.

CONDUCTING THE INTERVIEW

When considering the logistics of an interview, several factors are important:

(1) Arrangements for students to be interviewed should be made well in advance (at least one or two weeks), but allowance should be made for last minute changes in school or student schedules that can upset plans. In a school, interview schedules must be cleared with the principal, headmaster, teachers, and anyone else responsible for visitor protocol.

(2) Letters from parents may be required, and in any case it is good practice routinely to obtain permission from parents or guardians for interviewing minors. Usually, passive approval (that is, letters asking parents to contact a specific person only if they have questions or disapprove) will suffice, although some principals or governing boards require a signed letter of approval for each child. A sample letter is given in Appendix III.

(3) Although interviews will interrupt school schedules, care should be taken so that they cause as little disruption as possible. Some teachers will allow students to leave the room only in the morning or afternoon, or only during study halls, and their wishes should be respected. If school class periods are short (say 40 minutes), either the interviews can be shorter (12 to 15 minutes) or only one longer interview can be scheduled per period. Interviews should be timed so that they do not continue past recess, lunch, or dismissal times. Do not overschedule interviews; four to six a day is usually the most an interviewer can handle and stay alert, pleasant, and thorough. Teachers should be provided in advance with a list of students to be interviewed on each day.

(4) A small room should be chosen where there will be no interruptions and a minimum of background noise. In school settings this

space is often not easy to find, but usually there is at least one room available for part of the day, a book storage room, say, or a room near the mechanical facilities. Sometimes a private corner of a large room (such as a lunchroom) can work well.

(5) Unless interviews are in or close to the children's classroom, some arrangements need to be made for ushering students back and forth. One practice we have found successful is to usher the first student to the interview room and then to ask each student to usher the next student on the list. This gives the interviewer time to set up for the next person.

(6) A checklist of all materials needed for an interview should be prepared, as well as an "interview kit" containing all auxiliary materials, sheets for written answers, spare materials that might be needed, and so on. The interviewer should tick off each item on the checklist before leaving for the interview. (We guarantee that failure to do this will necessitate returning to home base after as few as 10 or 20 interviews.)

(7) Interviews should be recorded. Rarely have we found students who object, and, particularly when there are interesting auxiliary materials, they quickly forget the microphone. Lapel microphones are desirable when available. Inexpensive cassette tape recorders are now widely available, but we caution that some cheap audio cassettes fail to record, making them expensive in the long run. Video recording is desirable on occasion, when there is to be more than one interviewer, to standardize interview techniques and/or to train new interviewers. Written permission should be obtained to use either audio or video recordings. Photographic records (like Figure 7.5) can also be useful.

(8) The student's name should be recorded on the tape at the start of each interview, and all tapes, written sheets, and other materials labeled immediately afterward. A log should be kept of names, dates, times, and any anomalies that might be lost without these records.

In addition to logistic considerations, interviewers should be aware of a number of other problems and issues:

(1) *Interviewing should not be Socratic teaching.* We are trying to discern what students know and how they use that knowledge. It is tempting to ask, as Socrates might have done, questions that will steer students toward understanding, but this is a temptation that experienced teachers must struggle to avoid. Although the ability to learn new material is one indicator of prior knowledge and understanding, these interviews are designed for assessment, and using

Figure 7.5 Photographic record of an interview dealing with the physical nature of smells, showing the apparatus used and the setting.

them for teaching should be avoided as much as is possible. To accomplish this, it is a good idea for the interviewer to avoid positive or negative responses and to use neutral comments such as, I see. Tell me more about that. Is that all? Anything else you can tell me? Is this what you believe? (and then restate the student's claim). That is the same (or different) answer given to me by other students. Can you help me understand that better? and so on.

(2) *Interviewers must be thoroughly familiar with the material to be covered.* If they are competent in the relevant subject matter, people can be trained in a relatively short time to conduct effective interviews. It is impossible to probe, intelligently, a student's understanding if the interviewer has not spent years studying the field. Most interviews deal only with a narrow segment of subject matter that might be possible to master in a relatively short time, but only an interviewer who has a thorough knowledge of the field can respond

with appropriate follow-up questions or probes when interviewees give responses that may seem "wrong" or "meaningless" but are in fact interesting and creative when viewed from the broader perspective of the entire field.

(3) *Personality factors are important.* Interviewers who are either too aggressive or too timid may either bear down too hard on an interviewee or fail to probe enough to discover what the student really thinks about a topic. People with warm and accepting but reasonably demanding personalities make the best interviewers.

(4) *Interviewers must listen to the students they are interviewing.* It is easy not to "hear" a student's response because one is already preoccupied with the next question, or because the answer is different from what one expected to hear. A recording of a beginning interviewer is almost sure to reveal this happening at least once. Unfortunately, the same problem frequently occurs in ordinary teaching. One reason we recommend that all preservice teachers learn to conduct clinical interviews is that it helps them to learn to listen.

(5) *Patience is required.* Mary Budd Rowe (1974a and b), among others, has shown that most teachers allow a very short "wait-time" (less than one second) for an answer before they restate the question, ask another student to respond, or answer the question themselves. An interviewer should wait up to 10 or 15 seconds for a response (a pause that can indeed seem to be interminable!). On the other hand, the pause should not be too long; subjects will freeze up if they are stared at for as long as a minute or two. Students who do not respond in 5 or 10 seconds are usually too afraid or too unsure to give an answer, do not have one, or have not understood the question. A restructured question or a move to a new topic may be needed.

(6) *The interview atmosphere should be calm and relaxed.* Friendly greetings, smiles, and comments like "I'm confused about that; let's go on to something else," can help to ease the normal tension of an interview setting. Interviewers should try to project the image that they are human, too, and don't know all the answers.

(7) *Irrelevant discussion should be discouraged.* Some students will begin talking about their birthday party, a movie they once saw, or something else largely irrelevant to the interview. Because most of us rarely find anyone who will genuinely listen to us, all kinds of thoughts and feelings will often be "unloaded" on a good interviewer. Part of what makes interviewing exhausting is the constant tension between permitting and encouraging free cognitive expres-

sion and, at the same time, attempting to get interviewees to reveal what they know and how they think about a specific area of knowledge.

(8) *"I don't know," or "I forgot" answers seldom mean just that.* Most of the time, these answers (which we code as IDK responses) indicate that a student is not sufficiently clear or confident about the answer to give a substantive response. We may be probing an area of cognitive structure in which the student's concepts are not differentiated or integratively reconciled enough to permit the formation of specific propositional statements. When this happens, the question can be rephrased or a new aspect of the auxiliary material referred to in such a way as to permit new propositional linkages to operate. The concept map that was prepared for this segment of the interview can suggest new superordinate, subordinate, or cross linkages between related concepts. If no reasonable set of such probes (usually three or four alternatives at most) succeeds in producing substantive answers, it is best to make some reassuring comment to the interviewee and move on to a new set of questions (probing, as it were, a different area of cognitive structure).

(9) *Students vary widely in loquaciousness.* There are wide differences in the extent to which different students will respond and/or amplify answers to questions, and also wide variations in how the same student will respond on different subject matter or on different days. Although some of the techniques suggested in point (8) can be used to encourage "outflowing" from an interviewee's cognitive structure, important differences will remain.

(10) *Statements revealing feelings are significant.* Although we are describing primarily strategies for assessing cognitive structure, it is pertinent and valuable to request and record some of the student's feelings about the particular subject matter, relevant school experience, and so on. Often these affective responses will explain striking cognitive anomalies (for instance, "I love plants, but I hate reptiles and fish").

(11) *In sequential interviews, it can be helpful to refer to prior interviews and/or to relevant intervening instruction.* This usually encourages responsiveness on the part of the interviewee and helps to signal the area of cognitive structure to be "searched." Because of the severe time constraints, such references must necessarily be limited. When the interviewer is probing specifically for cross linking between two different conceptual domains, however, early reference to prior in-

terviews or instruction may encourage spontaneous expression of cross links or reveal important integrative reconciliations of concepts and/or misconceptions.

(12) *The student's own language should be used to rephrase questions or probe further.* Students often use colloquial, slang, or mispronounced words in their answers. To insist on the "right" word or pronunciation can be confusing, and may inhibit fuller expression of concepts and propositions. Students will sometimes use the wrong label (word) for the right concept (for example, students will often say that the earth is shaped like a circle, rather than a sphere). In these cases, they can be asked to explain the difference between the word they use and the correct concept label.

(13) *The interviewer's logic should not be forced upon the student.* Sometimes students will give inconsistent or illogical answers to "why" questions or "explain how" questions. They can be asked to clarify their reasoning, but they should not be expected to see the logical problems the interviewer sees in their answers. Occasionally, however, a student will recognize inconsistencies and clarify (integratively reconcile) concepts and propositional meanings during the course of the interview. Although every effort should be made to avoid imposing a teaching structure on an interview, probing questions will of course effect some meaningful learning.

(14) *Finally, interviews should end on a positive note.* This can be accomplished by thanking students for their help and commenting favorably on their cooperation, manner, and so on. An offer can be made to answer questions, but only if the student is not to be interviewed again in the near future on essentially the same subject matter. In any case, the interview should end with feelings that will make future interviews an experience to be welcomed and anticipated.

EVALUATING INTERVIEWS: CATEGORY SYSTEMS

Knowledge categories. In our early research with children, we used an approach whereby we classified students based on the knowledge they exhibited. Our interviews probed into how students used information, and we established categories to group students holding similar concepts and propositions about specific areas of science. Figures 7.6 and 7.7 show two of the category systems we developed. We continue to see value in using knowledge category systems; a consid-

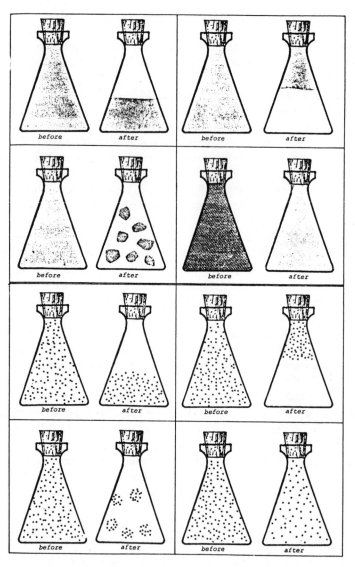

Figure 7.6 Pictorial representation of eight categories of responses given by eighth-grade children in an interview asking how the composition of air would change in a flask after half of the air was pumped out (lower right is the best response). [From Shimshon, Novick and Joseph Nussbaum, *Junior High School Pupils' Understanding of the Particulate Nature of Matter: An Interview Study*, Science Education, 62(3), 273-281 (1978). This figure appears as Figure III in this paper on page 279.]

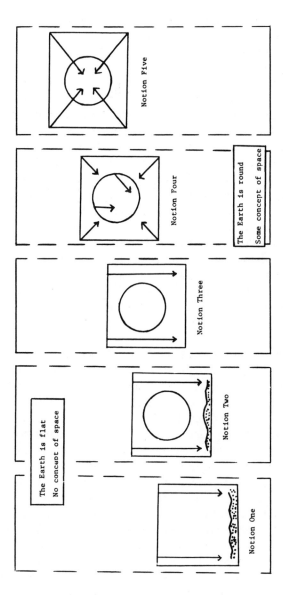

Figure 7.7 Five categories of responses identified in interviews about earth and gravity, showing second-grade students' variation in understanding from simple, child-centered "notion one," where all objects fall down (toward the floor), to "notion five," where gravity pulls objects toward the center of the Earth from any point on Earth (Nussbaum and Novak 1976).

erable amount of our current research uses some form of this approach for assessment.

To prepare a set of categories for classifying students' knowledge patterns, we began by listing characteristic misconceptions and valid propositions elicited in a set of interviews. About 20 to 30 interviews from the sample population are usually sufficient to generate enough statements to begin constructing a classification scheme. Our experience has been that 4 to 7 categories will usually encompass the typical responses given by students on the subject matter covered in a 15- to 30-minute interview. The statements are arranged into categories according to the validity of the concepts they are based upon: The lowest category comprises statements indicating the most misconceptions, the highest those based on the most valid propositions. Again, Figures 7.6 and 7.7 illustrate the categories constructed for two different interviews. After an initial set of categories is devised from the list of valid and invalid propositions offered by students, an attempt should be made to classify each student to determine if the categories are relatively discrete: Does each student fit reasonably well into one of the categories? If some responses place a given student in one category and other responses place the student in another, the category scheme needs to be reconsidered. A certain amount of trial and error is unavoidable, but we have always found it possible to establish a category system into which we could nicely fit 80 to 90 percent of our students. The remaining students can be placed in one category based on most of their responses, with the remainder of their responses fitting the next higher or lower category. Because cognitive development is a continuous process, it is inevitable that any category system for classifying student understanding of a subject will show a percentage of such "transitional" students.

One way to improve a category system is to interview students across a broad range of ages and/or abilities. A good category system will generally show that older or more able students tend to rank in "higher" categories (with more valid propositions) than younger or less able students. Because students' understanding of a subject area will be influenced in varying degrees by instruction and other experience, as well as by their general cognitive development, the percentage of students moving from "lower" to "higher" categories after instruction may not be constant over a given age range. Figure 7.8 shows the variation found in students' understanding of the concepts

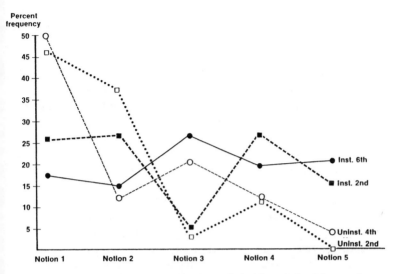

Figure 7.8 Percent of elementary school pupils holding each of five notions regarding Earth and gravity (see Figure 7.7). Data are shown for children without classroom instruction on these concepts (Uninst.) and for those who received instruction (Inst.) (Nussbaum 1983).

of Earth and gravity for various ages with and without instruction and illustrates a discontinuity in the rate of advance effected by good instruction in this area of knowledge.

Reasoning categories. In the beginning of this chapter, we noted the ingenious interviews designed by Piaget and his associates that led him to devise a theory of cognitive development identifying four basic types of cognitive operations, or reasoning categories. Piaget's system for classifying students' reasoning patterns based on this theory remains very popular with some educators, but the weight of evidence is moving increasingly toward the view that after the age of 30 or 36 months, all normal children possess essentially the same reasoning patterns as adults. What changes over time are the number of concepts and propositions they possess that are relevant to any interview task and the degree of hierarchial organization of those concepts and propositions (Novak 1977a, Donaldson 1978, Keil 1979, Macnamara 1982, Novak 1982, in press).

Developmental categories. William Perry (1970), working in the Bureau of Study Counsel at Harvard University, used a very open-ended interview format, not involving any tasks, in which students were asked to speak on experiences that stood out during the past school year. Perry found that the responses showed definite patterns as the students advanced from their freshman through their senior year. He devised nine "positions" or categories representing the maturation of students' world views from an "absolutist" view, where everything is right or wrong, good or bad (Position 1), to a legitimate uncertainty and diversity of opinion (Position 4), to a commitment to beliefs that will change and grow with maturation (Position 9). Perry's work has been criticized for the narrowness of the sample (Harvard male students enrolled 1963–67) and its consequent effect on the validity of his claims. We see value in Perry's work as it stands, however, as an example of interview methodology resulting in a scheme for categorizing maturation in world views. Kohlberg (1964), also at Harvard, constructed a category system for moral development, but we have grave reservations about both his methodologies and his inferences (see Gilligan 1982).

CONCEPT-MAPPING EVALUATION

In Chapter 2, we noted that concept mapping was first used in our research programs at Cornell University to evaluate growth in children's understanding of scientific concepts as a result of audio-tutorial instruction. It was later possible to construct concept maps for groups of related audio-tutorial lessons[2] and then to use these maps as references for analyzing responses given by children in interviews covering the same subjects as the lessons. Figure 5.1 is an example of such a concept map, constructed by Richard Rowell (1978) using the template shown.

If the interview is designed from a concept map, as we have suggested, a "template" concept map exists that can now be used to construct students' *cognitive maps*.[3] From a transcript of the inter-

---

2 At the time the audio-tutorial lessons were developed (1965–72), we had not begun using concept maps for instructional planning through clinical interviews.

3 We use the term *cognitive map* to indicate a representation of what we believe to be the organization of concepts and propositions in a given student's cognitive structure. Cognitive maps are idiosyncratic, whereas concept maps should represent an area of knowledge in a way that experts in that field agree is valid. Experts

view, a cognitive map that shows the concepts and propositions each student evidenced in the interview is constructed over the template of the original concept map for the interview.

One drawback of this approach is our tendency to see only what we want to see in a student's response. By applying as the major criterion for the student's understanding the same concept map framework upon which the interview was designed, creative or unanticipated ways to view the same subject matter can be missed. We have not, however, found this to be a major problem. Evaluators who have a thorough knowledge of the subject matter area covered can easily recognize student responses that show good understanding even though they do not fit into the template concept map for the interview, and in any case this occurs infrequently (with 10 percent or less of the students interviewed). One can adjust the ratings for such students by using the scoring criteria given in Table 2.4. In fact, any student whose cognitive map departs radically from the established concept map can be reassessed on the basis of those criteria, independently of the template map.

Whenever concept mapping approaches are used to interpret interviews, certain key psychological and epistemological ideas must be kept in mind. Because knowledge in any field is constantly changing, concept maps constructed as the basis for interview planning and/or interview interpretation will always be somewhat behind the current state of knowledge. There is always some disagreement among experts as to what set of propositions best describes current views in any area of knowledge. In addition, "circularity" – seeing only what our "goggles" permit us to see – is a problem. As Kuhn (1962) put it, our paradigms are the goggles through which we see the world; as these paradigms change, so do our views of records or events. We see Kuhn's views as too simplistic, and prefer more contemporary views of epistemology that see complex and competing frameworks of theory and methodology operating to construct new meanings and new knowledge (see Toulmin 1972, Brown 1979). Meanings are idiosyncratic by nature – all of our perceptions are influenced by the concepts and propositions we hold in our cognitive structures, and we see the world as our cognitive frameworks permit us to see it.

will disagree on details of a concept map for any given body of knowledge – partly because views of key concepts in any field change constantly with new research – but most will concede that a well-devised concept map is a reasonable representation.

Even so, the patterns and frameworks through which individuals or "experts" report on the meanings of events or objects they observe are remarkably stable. And it is partly for this reason that Vee diagramming and concept mapping can be useful as evaluation methodologies.

CONCEPT PROPOSITIONAL ANALYSIS (CPA)

Another method for evaluating interviews is what we call *concept propositional analysis (CPA)*,[4] which is based on the psychological notion that the meaning of any concept for a student is shown by the set of propositions that a student constructs incorporating the concept. The technique involves editing an interview to determine the sets of propositions generated by a given student to specific questions. The first step is to identify, from the transcript, all propositional assertions made by the student. Some sentences may contain several propositions, or words may need to be added so that statements reflect meanings in terms of the questions asked. If CPA is applied both before and after instruction, a table can be constructed to show (1) the propositions given by a student to sets of questions before instruction, (2) the key propositions presented or illustrated in the instruction, and (3) the propositions given by a student to the same questions after instruction. Table 7.2 is an example.

CPA has an advantage over concept mapping and cognitive mapping in that it takes all propositions generated by a student at face value, without imposing a predetermined structure on them. (The predetermined structure of the interview obviously influences what propositions the students construct, but the propositional statements are not subsequently interpolated onto a concept map.) CPA is a useful technique in studies of long-term changes in a given student's cognitive framework. It is also useful to teachers, for the starting point in instruction should be the set of propositions held by students. As we have already pointed out, many of the students' propositions will indicate misconceptions or inadequate specificity of concept meanings that can then be the teacher's source for plan-

---

4 Concept propositional analysis is a label we used to distinguish our work from that of grammarians and others interested in language construction rather than the psychology of learning. Sentence diagrams, phrase analysis, and similar grammatical analysis deals with different issues than we are concerned with here.

Table 7.2. *Comparison of propositions from pre- and postinstruction interviews and key statements from relevant intervening instruction*[a]

Preinstruction interview	Instruction	Postinstruction interview
Real seeds are alive because you can squeeze real seeds but you can't squeeze phoney ones.[a]	You are going to grow these corn seeds.	These are seeds, they're alive.[a]
Alive means things are squeezable.	Corn seeds need water to grow.	I don't know if *these* seeds are alive.
Alive doesn't mean anything else.	How can you get these corn seeds to grow?	I think they [the seeds] are dead.
Like if these seeds were alive you could squeeze them.	If this corn seed is alive, and you put water in the bottle, it will probably start to grow.	They [seeds] won't grow alone.
	When a seed starts to grow you know that it is alive.	There is nothing you can do to make them [seeds] grow because they might be dead and if they're dead they won't grow.
	How will you know if a seed is alive?	To check if they [the seeds] are alive, you have to wait for a few days and if there's water, light and air they *might* grow into big plants.
	When you see a seed start to grow, you will know that the seed is alive.	If they [seeds] grow, they're alive.
	Seeds that are alive grow.	
	A plant needs water and air and light.	
	You must watch the seeds that you planted and see if they grow.	

Table 7.2. (*cont.*)

Some of the seeds are alive because you can see them grow.

This corn seed is alive because it's growing.

The corn seed must be with water and air and light to change and grow into a large corn plant.

[a] Statements made by the student are given in the order in which they appeared in the transcript of the interview. *Source:* From Pines 1977 (Case study 1: a "sophisticated" response).

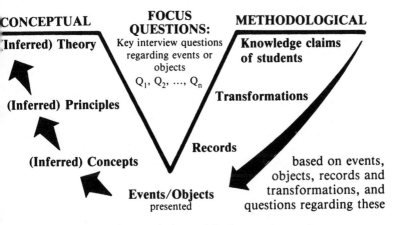

CONCEPTUAL

(Inferred) Theory

(Inferred) Principles

(Inferred) Concepts

FOCUS QUESTIONS:
Key interview questions regarding events or objects
$Q_1, Q_2, ..., Q_n$

METHODOLOGICAL

Knowledge claims of students

Transformations

Records

Events/Objects
presented

based on events, objects, records and transformations, and questions regarding these

Figure 7.9 The Vee, when used as a tool for interpreting student responses in an interview, is read from knowledge claims (statements made by the student) to events presented to construct inferences about concepts, principles, and theories held by the student.

ning and encouraging explicit discussions, demonstrations, and negotiations of meanings during classwork. In programmed audio-tutorial modules or computer-aided instruction, CPA can be a valuable adjunct to concept maps for instructional program planning.

GOWIN'S VEE ANALYSIS

We can consider that the propositions a student makes in response to questions are that student's knowledge claims based on his or her interpretation of the objects or events and data provided. Given a fixed set of events or objects and questions, we can infer what concepts, principles, and perhaps theories the student is using to make a knowledge claim. Figure 7.9 shows the general model for the application of this technique.

This technique for interview analysis is in many ways a composite of other techniques, with the Vee heuristic used to organize student responses. To apply the technique it is first necessary to construct a concept map for the interview to represent the ideal map an expert might use to interpret the objects or events presented to the students (we assume that interviews also contain auxiliary materials). In most interviews, numerous questions are posed, and it is somewhat of an interpretation problem to reduce these many questions to one or a few focus questions. This is seldom the major problem, however, as interviews are usually designed to deal with one or a few major questions (to do otherwise would make the interview process ambiguous or superficial). The principal difficulties in interpretation arise as one attempts to work "down and across" the Vee from the claims (propositions) made by the student to make reasonable inferences about the type of cognitive map that would lead a student to make such claims. Figure 7.10 is an example of an idealized concept map prepared for analysis of interviews dealing with the molecular structure of matter and Figure 7.11 shows the results from an analysis of an interview with a second-grade child. The technique has been applied in many fields: Figure 7.12 is a concept map inferred from an interview with an advanced graduate student in music composition and Figure 7.13 was prepared from an interview with a beginning student in music composition.

Despite its difficulties, the Vee analysis technique has significant merit. For educational purposes, it is stimulating to display a set of claims on an overhead projector and then discuss and debate what cognitive frameworks could reasonably have led to these claims given the events or objects and data observed. The use of the Vee analysis technique turns Piagetian reasoning claims upside down because it assumes that students of any age may *appear* to be preoperational, concrete operational, or formal thinkers depending on the adequacy of their relevant conceptual frameworks. We assume that students are rational thinkers, and that nearly all students are capable of what Piaget called fully formal operational thinking if they have an adequate framework of relevant concepts. Our research, and our interpretation of other research findings, supports this assumption. From age 4 or 5 to senescence, the major factor influencing students' construction of knowledge claims is the adequacy of their relevant cognitive structures, including their ability to use certain general strategies for attacking specific problem areas (see Novak 1977b). Accepting the validity of the Vee technique for analyzing educational interviews means repudiating in large part the Piagetian notion of stages of cognitive development. Our counsel to the skeptic is, Try it and see for yourself. So far the colleagues we have worked with are persuaded that our alternative explanatory theory is at least as valid as

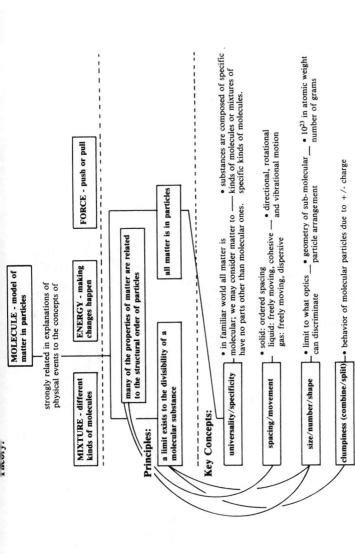

Figure 7.10 A concept map constructed for use as a template for interpreting interviews with children regarding the molecular structure of matter. Concepts, principles, and theories held by the children, inferred by using the technique illustrated in Figure 7.9. Results are shown in Figure 7.11 (Ault, Novak, and Gowin, in press).

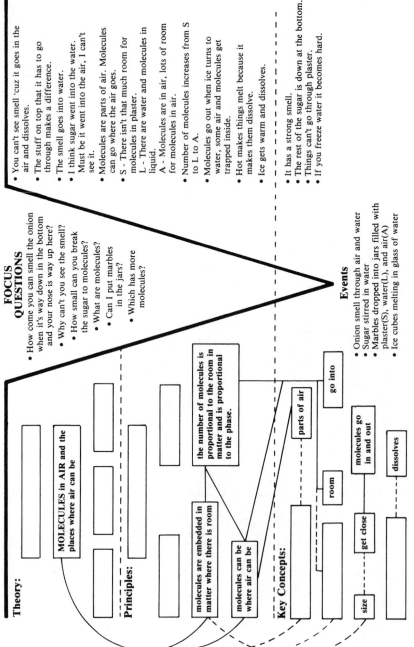

Theory:

MOLECULES in AIR and the places where air can be

Principles:

molecules are embedded in matter where there is room

molecules can be where air can be

the number of molecules is proportional to the room in matter and is proportional to the phase.

Key Concepts:

size

get close

molecules go in and out

dissolves

room

parts of air

go into

FOCUS QUESTIONS

• How come you can smell the onion when it's way down in the bottom and your nose is way up here?
• Why can't you see the smell?
• How small can you break the sugar to molecules?
• What are molecules?
• Can I put marbles in the jars?
• Which has more molecules?

• You can't see smell 'cuz it goes in the air and dissolves.
• The stuff on top that it has to go through makes a difference.
• The smell goes into water.
• I think sugar went into the water. Must be it went into the air, I can't see it.
• Molecules are parts of air. Molecules can go where the air goes.
• S - There isn't that much room for molecules in plaster.
  L - There are water and molecules in liquid.
  A - Molecules are in air, lots of room for molecules in air.
• Number of molecules increases from S to L to A.
• Molecules go out when ice turns to water, some air and molecules get trapped inside.
• Hot makes things melt because it makes them dissolve.
• Ice gets warm and dissolves.

• It has a strong smell.
• The rest of the sugar is down at the bottom.
• Things can't go through plaster.
• If you freeze water it becomes hard.

Events

• Onion smell through air and water
• Sugar stirred in water
• Marbles dropped into jars filled with plaster(S), water(L), and air(A)
• Ice cubes melting in glass of water

Figure 7.11 A Vee showing questions, key statements, and inferences made from an interview with a second-grade child

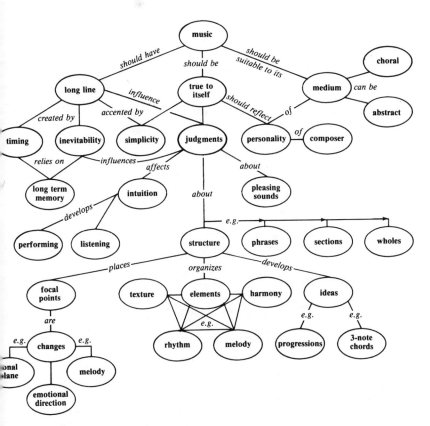

Figure 7.12 A concept map made from an interview with an experienced composer and PhD student in music composition. Music composed by this musician is characterized by his emphasis on unity, with segments of the composition showing harmonious and natural connectedness.

Piagetian theory, and other recent work supports this view (Keil 1979, Macnamara 1982).

SUMMARY

It should now be evident that there are no simple recipes for evaluating interviews. We can understand why behaviorist psychologists rooted in an empirical tradition find interviews at best unsatisfying for evaluating human behavior. We must remember, however, that

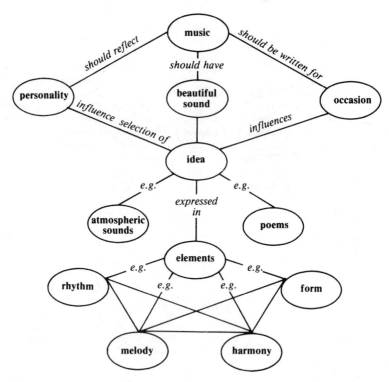

Figure 7.13 A concept map prepared from an interview with a beginning student of composition. This person had less knowledge of music than an expert and therefore placed major stress on the music "sounding right."

as teachers and learners we are not seeking absolute truths, but rather a better understanding of how the world works. We believe that interviews, as well as the evaluation strategies described in this chapter, can help educators and researchers who seek to understand better how humans make sense of the world as they perceive it.

8

IMPROVING EDUCATIONAL RESEARCH

E DUCATIONAL RESEARCH, like research in any field, is an attempt to create new knowledge. Not all research succeeds in producing knowledge claims that contribute to increasing human understanding, and educational research has been notoriously unproductive in this respect. We believe that many of the past failures of educational research, as well as research in other social sciences, are due partly to the *artifactual* nature of educational events or objects, which are not naturally occurring but rather produced by people. Naturally occurring events, not being subject to the vagaries of human individuality, are much more consistent and predictable. It is not surprising that more progress has been made in astronomy, physics, chemistry, biology, and geology than in sociology or education. The historical sequence of disciplinary advances corresponds roughly to the regularity of the naturally occurring events or objects being studied and how easily they can be observed. Photosynthesis and continental movements are both very regular events, but it has taken decades to develop the concepts and methods to observe them. All disciplines are also dependent upon the concepts humans invent to be able to see regularities, even in naturally occurring phenomena.

In Chapter 1 we indicated that we will not dwell on the issue of whether or not education is a science. Learning and the construction of knowledge are both naturally occurring phenomena, and at least some aspects of education have natural regularity (some of its aspects, such as school organization, have at times a distressing stability as well). But one of the reasons we believe education can be much improved is that, because it is artifactual and therefore highly dependent on the choices people make, we can choose to modify educational events at will. What we need is a vastly increased body of knowledge to guide us in the choices we make. The proper role for educational research is to construct this body of knowledge.

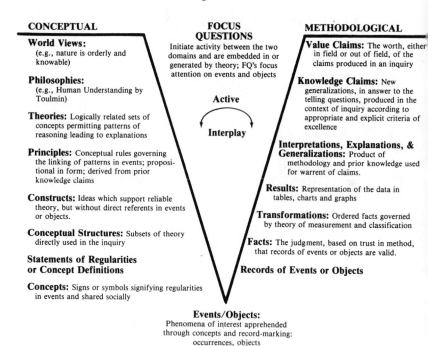

CONCEPTUAL

FOCUS QUESTIONS

METHODOLOGICAL

World Views: (e.g., nature is orderly and knowable)

Philosophies: (e.g., Human Understanding by Toulmin)

Theories: Logically related sets of concepts permitting patterns of reasoning leading to explanations

Principles: Conceptual rules governing the linking of patterns in events; propositional in form; derived from prior knowledge claims

Constructs: Ideas which support reliable theory, but without direct referents in events or objects.

Conceptual Structures: Subsets of theory directly used in the inquiry

Statements of Regularities or Concept Definitions

Concepts: Signs or symbols signifying regularities in events and shared socially

FOCUS QUESTIONS Initiate activity between the two domains and are embedded in or generated by theory; FQ's focus attention on events and objects

Active

Interplay

Records of Events or Objects

Value Claims: The worth, either in field or out of field, of the claims produced in an inquiry

Knowledge Claims: New generalizations, in answer to the telling questions, produced in the context of inquiry according to appropriate and explicit criteria of excellence

Interpretations, Explanations, & Generalizations: Product of methodology and prior knowledge used for warrent of claims.

Results: Representation of the data in tables, charts and graphs

Transformations: Ordered facts governed by theory of measurement and classification

Facts: The judgment, based on trust in method, that records of events or objects are valid.

Events/Objects: Phenomena of interest apprehended through concepts and record-marking: occurrences, objects

Figure 8.1 The Vee heuristic with descriptions of the interacting elements involved in the construction or analysis of knowledge in any discipline. Although all elements are involved in any coherent research program, the major sources of difficulty in individual inquiries usually begin at the bottom of the Vee, where concepts, events/objects, and records must be scrutinized. (See also the simpler version shown in Figure 1.2.)

In the past, educational researchers borrowed theories and methods from other disciplines such as psychology, sociology, and philosophy. Although it is useful to observe how theories and methodologies in other fields serve to construct new knowledge, education involves a unique set of phenomena, and a discipline of education must construct its own theories and methods. We have moved toward this end in earlier theoretical writings (Novak 1977, Gowin 1981); this book represents our first major effort to put forth complementary conceptions and new methodologies.

Viewed in terms of the Vee heuristic, a discipline must strive to build its own conceptual-theoretical framework, which in turn can lead to new ways to view and record educational events and to ways to construct new kinds of educational events (concept mapping instruction, for example). This is shown schematically in Figure 8.1. When the construction of such events is guided by theory and concepts that are distinctively educational, new kinds of records, such as Vee diagrams for segments of curriculum, and new kinds of transformations can be made, leading to knowledge claims that move the field forward. With theory-guided construction of new events and new knowledge claims, which operate gradually to allow existing concepts, principles, and theories to be modified or discarded, the discipline becomes "event-centered." It becomes, in Conant's (1947) terms, a progressive enterprise.

A word of caution is in order. Educating is a complex activity, and we must remain flexible in how we choose to construct educational events and in how we interpret these events. Time, talent, and funding are as necessary in educational research as they are in any other discipline. So far, most of our research has been done by graduate students in training rather than by professional scholars. Novices have the virtue of not knowing in advance what will not work, and many inquiries of our students have been marked by a release of creative energy. Their interests have been diverse, resulting in inquiries about educating in music, nursing, mathematics, peace studies, literature, foreign languages, science, sports, counseling, hotel management, history, and medicine. In all of these fields, we have found the Vee heuristic to be valuable for organizing and interpreting research in the framework of the theory we have been developing.

THEORY-DRIVEN RESEARCH

A field of inquiry becomes a discipline when it is guided by its own theory and methodologies. By this criterion, most of the work in educational research over the past eighty years has not been derived from a disciplinary framework. Nevertheless, there have been numerous studies observing and recording classroom events, and some laboratory research, that have laid a groundwork for the construction of at least a rudimentary theory of educating. Over the past decade, as our own theoretical views have taken shape, we have found that our research studies have become progressively more focused, more creative and more cumulative. Each piece of research has added to our understanding of or skill in using new methodologies and interpreting the meaning of records obtained by applying new meth-

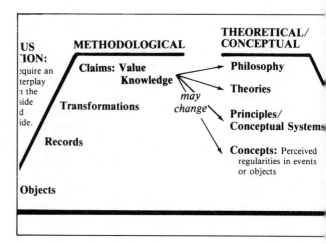

Figure 8.2 The "parade of Vees" schema illustrating that knowledge construction is a continuous process wherein new knowledge contributes new concepts, principles, and theories (or modifications in existing ones) and thus influences further inquiries.

ods. Increasingly, our graduate students have found it necessary and valuable to read theses recently completed by students working within our theoretical framework, and also to test the power of this framework against the methodologies used by other research groups. We see our program advancing as a kind of "parade of Vees," as is shown schematically in Figure 8.2.

Studies focused on the facilitation of classroom learning received a strong positive impetus when we began to apply the cognitive learning theory first proposed by David Ausubel (1963). For almost a century, the dominant views in psychology were shaped by Pavlov's early work with dogs and the work of Watson, Skinner, and others, also with animals. The theories developed by these "behaviorists" were used to design events, or experiments, to change the overt and observable behavior of dogs, cats, pigeons, and mice. Consequently, thousands of new events were made to happen; they were observed and recorded, and data transformations were produced, in what was called the science of behavior. It is not surprising that psychologists working within this framework should have dominated the discipline, for they were proceeding in a systematic fashion to create new knowledge, knowledge that could then be recreated (con-

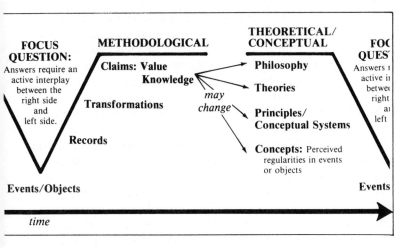

firmed) by other psychologists using similar methods. It is also not surprising that success in the study of animal behavior should have led to the extension of the same concepts, theories, and methods to the study of human behavior. In some respects, the extension to humans was warranted and useful. But the most significant aspect of human behavior is our ability to form concepts, to label concepts with language symbols, and to manipulate these symbols; and it was this fundamental difference in human thinking and learning that rendered inappropriate the wholesale application of theories and methodologies developed from animal learning experiments or human behavior experiments that did not center on the use of concepts. A new discipline of human conceptual or cognitive learning was needed.

There were early pioneers who recognized the fundamental differences between animal learning (or rote recall human learning of material such as nonsense syllables) and the learning or thinking that characterizes, for example, human problem solving. But because their concepts were necessarily fuzzy at first and their methodologies less replicable than those of the behaviorists, the work of these pioneers was largely ignored in North America, and the net effect was a form of coercion or censorship that may have limited the growth of cognitive psychology here. Jean Piaget, working in Switzerland, became the most prominent researcher in human cognitive studies, but most of his work was limited to understanding differences in cognitive functioning at various ages, and was not concerned with cognitive learning per se (see Piaget 1926). In 1954, Norbert Wiener, a brilliant mathematician, proposed a cybernetic model for human learning based on his work with self-regulating mechanical systems, although this theoretical framework did not become popular until the late 1970s. Since then, more elaborate information-processing models of human cognitive functioning have been devised, but these models, from our perspective, remain rooted in the epistemology of computer, or machine, functioning – and are consequently of less long-term promise than cognitive psychologies modeled on how humans construct, acquire, and use concepts in the various disciplines. Partly because the computer metaphor on which they are based does not involve feelings, these new cognitive science models also fail to connect thinking with feeling.

In addition to cognitive learning, students acquire attitudes, values, and skills. There has been no adequate theory of attitude learning, nor has there been a theory of value and skill learning. We have been working to fashion a theory of educating that deals with all of these dimensions of human experience. A comprehensive theory of educating must deal with thinking, feeling, and acting and address all four commonplaces of educating: teaching, learning, curriculum, and governance. *Educating* (Gowin 1981) is the first work we know about that attempts to present a theoretical view that embraces all of these elements. In *Educating,* combined with ideas from Ausubel (1968, 1978) and Novak (1977a), we have a theoretical framework that now permits disciplinary study of the whole spectrum of educational problems. What is needed are far more educational research teams who engage in theory-driven research, based either on our framework or on other explicitly stated theoretical views.

RESEARCH PROPOSALS

Students' work. Our graduate students now routinely construct a Vee diagram to present their research proposals and have found it very helpful. Decisions about what students ought to do follow directly from Vee analysis, for it is easy to see what is missing – and thus what next needs to be done – and also because the Vee analysis clarifies where linkages are strong, the student can stop worrying about these areas. The dreaded doctoral oral examination becomes less anxiety producing when students realize they can defend their dissertations by using the guidance that comes from the Vee analyses. If they can articulate the relations the Vee diagram requires, all relevant questions have a justifiable answer in terms of elements on the Vee or interactions between these elements.

For faculty, the Vee analysis is an efficient way to see the substance of an inquiry. A whole thesis study can be summarized diagrammatically on one page. The Vee has become the key visual prop in lectures and seminars in our research group, and we suggest that other groups try using this heuristic in a similar manner.

SELECTING A RESEARCH PROBLEM

Many graduate students struggle with the question of what research problem to select. This is a legitimate question in any discipline, but in educational research, it has been for many students an agonizing one. Unlike those in the sciences and some of the social sciences, few graduate students in education become involved in programmatic research. It would be unheard of for students in physics, chemistry, or biology to go off on their own to work on a research problem in which both concepts and methodologies were unrelated to the work being done by their colleagues. These disciplines have established sets of concepts and data-gathering methodologies, with demonstrated success in producing new knowledge, that no graduate student could hope to replicate alone.

By contrast, it is not uncommon for five graduate students in education working with the same professor to be addressing five different, methodologically unrelated problems! Are graduate students in education such creative, extraordinary people? Not likely. What is happening is that too many graduate students, like many others involved in educational research, are simply randomly searching for a major formula to achieve some marvelous educational result. Non-programmatic research in education, where our work is made even more difficult by the artifactual nature of the events and objects we study, is no more likely to reveal new knowledge than are astrology or reading tea leaves. (Though, unfortunately, some educators do believe that astrology and reading tea leaves can generate knowledge claims! To these people we have nothing to offer.)

We will assume, therefore, that any educational inquiry must be rooted in a set of evolving concepts, principles, and theories regarding teaching, learning, curriculum, and governance, as well as an established (but hopefully also evolving) set of data-gathering and data-transforming processes. The problem of choosing a specific research problem then reduces to such questions as

(1) What are the significant educational aspects of the events chosen to be studied?

(2) What conceptual difficulties can best be addressed by the existing research methodologies of the research group?

(3) What aspects of the principles or theories guiding the inquiries are most in need of further empirical testing?

(4) What possibilities (for example, the microcomputer revolution) exist for creating significant new educational events, and how can such new events be constructed to test or modify the concepts or theories guiding the inquiries?

(5) What new record-making and record-transforming methods could be applied to "standard" educational events? (Videotaping, computer records of learner errors, concept mapping, and modified Piagetian interviews are a few examples.)

(6) What new data transformation techniques can be applied to data of the type the group gathers? (In the past, we would have answered chi-square analysis, Gosset's t test, analysis of variance, and, more recently, multivariate analytic tests and meta-analysis, but this book adds new techniques to our repertoire.)

(7) Are there new ways to generate new knowledge claims from standard data-gathering or data-transforming methodologies? (Using the Vee heuristic would be one way.)

(8) Are there concepts, theories, and/or methodologies in other disciplines that can be applied either to create new educational events or to generate new research questions? (Our bias here leans in favor of concepts and methodologies from ecology, ethology, and anthropology, but concepts or methodologies could be transferred from any discipline.)

(9) What social-political issues of current importance can be used to define new research questions, questions that can be legitimately addressed by the concepts and methodologies of the research group? (Questions regarding the effectiveness of Head Start programs would be a good example.)

(10) Can enough financial and/or school support be generated to sustain a research program? Research costs money, and most graduate students and professors cannot ignore this issue. Compared with space, atomic energy, or cancer research (to say nothing about weapons research), educational research gets almost no funding, so that educational researchers are usually starving for support. The basic problem is that we cannot expect to get more support for educational research from public or private sources until we demonstrate a better research track record. Educational research has not been known for its practical yield, so how can we persuade the public to support this work? We noted some of the reasons for this problem at the beginning of this chapter. We hope this book may help to resolve the dilemma in time.

(11) Is it right to pursue this kind of inquiry? This question is a value question, and not easy to answer. Its corollaries are, Do we have the right to intervene in children's or teachers' lives in the ways demanded by the events we wish to construct? Is this fair to the children's parents or to the community, social group, or other relevant constituencies? What could be the long-term negative outcome of our intervention?

(12) Finally, and perhaps most important, a researcher must ask, Is this question important to me? Do I care about it? Is this something I believe in? Is this something I feel is worth doing? Without personal commitment, it is unlikely that any educational research study will contribute to knowledge. Education is a difficult field of inquiry – one has to believe in what one is doing if one expects to contribute to human understanding in this field. Education is a moral enterprise. The usual expectations of research to predict and control events are constrained by the fact that we must respect persons, and their right to think differently and to choose freely. This is one of the fundamental differences between the human and the natural sciences.

CREATING NEW EDUCATIONAL EVENTS

Productive ideas for events or objects to be observed derive from existing concepts or theories of the discipline. In what Kuhn (1962) called the "preparadigm" stage (without major guiding principles) of a field of study, the only recourse for investigators is to gather observations carefully. Once a paradigm or major explanatory principle is invented by a creative leader in the field, research is guided by the paradigm and progress in creating knowledge accelerates.

Learning how to learn

Throughout most of the past century, educational research could best be described as preparadigmatic. The possible exceptions to this were studies, common until the 1960s, that adopted the behavioral paradigm so popular in psychology and applied to educational research. Behavioral psychological theory, however, expressly ignores or denies the idiosyncratic, covert concept meanings that are the principal factors in most human learning. The overt repression in education of research studies not employing the behavioral paradigm is one reason educational research has been slow in advancing.

Lacking paradigms to guide the creation of educational events that emphasized meaningful learning, educational researchers borrowed data transformation techniques from other fields. Throughout the 1960s, an educational research report that did not contain sophisticated multivariate statistical analysis was not easy to get published. The leading educational research journals published thousands of reports that employed elegant statistics, often in ways that violated key assumptions underlying the use of these statistics. The educational events observed, unfortunately, were usually not constructed from insights derived from educational principles (with the result that the knowledge claims from such studies either concluded that there were no statistically significant differences between the control and experimental groups, or were claims that could not be used to further the development of educational principles). The disenchantment with this kind of research that set in by the late 1970s has led to somewhat greater openness to alternative research approaches in education. With new theoretical insights on the nature of human learning and epistemology, we expect to see education emerge as a recognized discipline with frameworks of theories, principles, and concepts guiding our educational practices by the year 2000.[1]

---

1 There is the danger of a new dogma sweeping educational research, a dogma rooted in the epistemology of computer data storage and processing but applied to human cognitive performance. "Modern cognitive science," as it is immodestly labeled, claims that "rigorous" research can be done on human learning, data storage and processing, and problem solving. In many respects, this new orthodoxy is a reincarnation of behaviorist views that ignore the idiosyncratic nature of human concept understandings and the role these meanings play in new learning and problem solving. This research is driven by an epistemology of empiricism, rather than the constructivist epistemology now widely held by philosophers and theorists.

A comprehensive theory guiding research in education must deal with all four commonplaces: teaching, learning, curriculum, and governance. The selection or construction of educational events for research requires first narrowing the inquiry to center on one of the four commonplaces. Since events central to each commonplace are influenced by the nature of the other three, however, we cannot hope to isolate one or a few variables and ignore (or control) everything else. This is one reason educational research is so much more difficult than research in physics or biology. For example, if we choose to focus attention on how concept mapping may influence students' transition toward more meaningful learning patterns, thus centering on the learning commonplace, we must also modify teaching practices; then concept mapping becomes part of the new curriculum, and time must be allocated for concept mapping activities (a change in governance). Because we cannot isolate variables in educating in any valid way, we are always confronted with complex problems regarding the meaning of the records and transformed records we produce. This is why we believe theory to be essential for progress in educational research, and why the Vee heuristic can be a powerful tool.

Figures 8.3 to 8.6 are Vees constructed for some of the research projects carried out at Cornell University. The examples were selected to show studies focused primarily on questions regarding teaching (Figure 8.3), learning (Figure 8.4), curriculum (Figure 8.5), and governance (Figure 8.6). It should be evident from these Vee diagrams, however, that, at least to some extent, each study involved consideration of all four commonplaces.

We have found that changes in instructional practices that depart widely from the common patterns requiring largely rote recall of information are not welcomed by some students. Approximately 5 to 20 percent of students respond negatively to instruction that requires meaningful learning. These students will resent requirements for concept mapping and Vee diagramming. About the same percentage of students find these strategies help them to do "just what they were trying to do" and are enthusiastic. The majority of students tend to respond somewhat negatively at first and then become more positive as they gain competence and confidence in the new strategies. As a result, and because learning strategies (and testing practices) need to be changed for the majority of students, not just a segment, initial

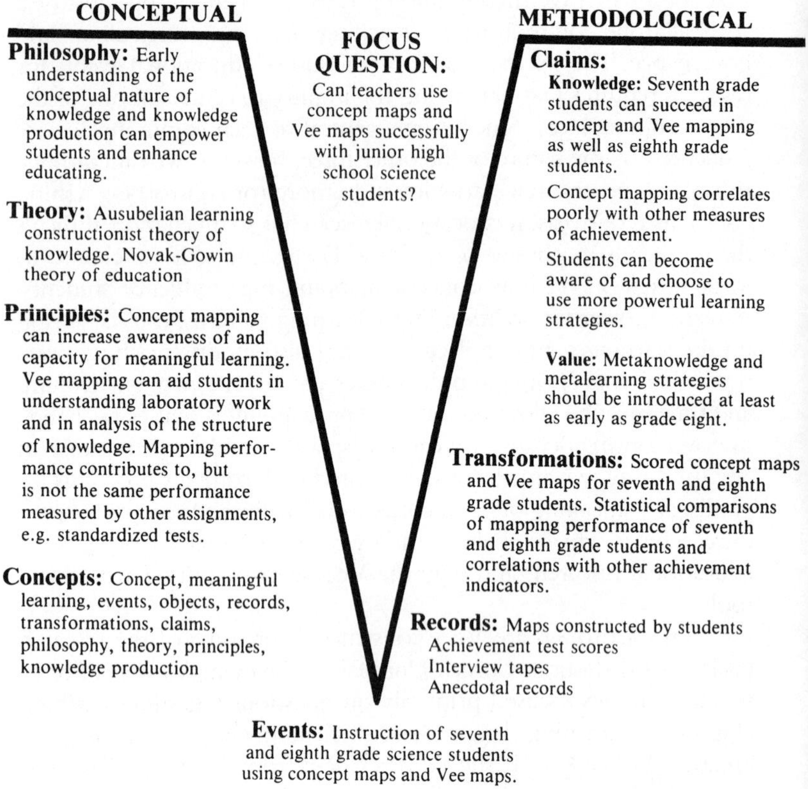

CONCEPTUAL

FOCUS QUESTION:

METHODOLOGICAL

Philosophy: Early understanding of the conceptual nature of knowledge and knowledge production can empower students and enhance educating.

Can teachers use concept maps and Vee maps successfully with junior high school science students?

Claims:

Knowledge: Seventh grade students can succeed in concept and Vee mapping as well as eighth grade students.

Concept mapping correlates poorly with other measures of achievement.

Theory: Ausubelian learning constructionist theory of knowledge. Novak-Gowin theory of education

Students can become aware of and choose to use more powerful learning strategies.

Principles: Concept mapping can increase awareness of and capacity for meaningful learning. Vee mapping can aid students in understanding laboratory work and in analysis of the structure of knowledge. Mapping performance contributes to, but is not the same performance measured by other assignments, e.g. standardized tests.

Value: Metaknowledge and metalearning strategies should be introduced at least as early as grade eight.

Transformations: Scored concept maps and Vee maps for seventh and eighth grade students. Statistical comparisons of mapping performance of seventh and eighth grade students and correlations with other achievement indicators.

Concepts: Concept, meaningful learning, events, objects, records, transformations, claims, philosophy, theory, principles, knowledge production

Records: Maps constructed by students
Achievement test scores
Interview tapes
Anecdotal records

Events: Instruction of seventh and eighth grade science students using concept maps and Vee maps.

Figure 8.3 Vee diagram of the study of teaching concept mapping and Vee making to junior high school science students. Although this study dealt primarily with the effectiveness of teaching strategies, questions of learning, curriculum, and governance were also considered (see Novak, Gowin, and Johansen 1983).

achievement scores on typical multiple choice or short-answer tests will be lower on the average for classes using meaningful learning strategies for six or eight weeks and then will continually improve. These effects on average scores are shown schematically in Figure 8.7. Teachers and researchers introducing new meaningful learning strategies should be prepared for this initial period of learning adjustment and the attendant feelings. When groups are compared over a semester, it is commonly observed that overall test performance has been about equal for students given standard instruction and those who received instruction emphasizing meaningful learning. On tests requiring transfer problem solving, however, groups learning meaningfully will usually show significant gains, and these gains increase over time (Novak, Gowin, and Johansen 1983; Novak in press).

Most educational research continues to be "method driven"; that is, the studies are based primarily on the use of some test or record-making device, statistical procedure (such as meta-analysis), or combination of these to answer stereotyped questions. Recent studies on why males outperform females, or are "overrepresented," in scientific and mathematical fields (see Fennema and Sherman 1977, Benbow and Stanley 1982, 1983) are an example of this kind of research. With no theory to guide the inquiry, data collected from thousands of students led Benbow and Stanley (1983) to conclude that they do not know why males outperform females by as much as 13 to 1 in SAT mathematics scores. Our "theory-driven" studies show that a possible explanation, which is supported by both Benbow and Stanley's and our own data, is the different school socialization of males and females: Females are more acquiescent, and accept the primarily rote learning patterns characteristic of much school learning, whereas males more frequently use the more meaningful learning strategies necessary for success in complex problem solving in strongly hierarchical disciplines such as mathematics. Figure 8.8 shows our theory-based model schematically.

DATA GATHERING

Graduate students also often ask, What kind of data should I collect? or How much data do I need for a (Master's or PhD) thesis? These are not the relevant questions. The important questions are

(1) What records of events are the key to the conceptual and/or theoretical issues with which we are concenred?
(2) What kind of record(s) does our work situation and knowledge best qualify us to gather?
(3) What records might lead to our being able to make substantiated claims about the events we are interested in?
(4) What new record-making ideas or technology can we apply to our research question(s)?

CONCEPTUAL

Philosophy:

Knowledge is an evolving population of concepts.

Knowledge is a product of inquiry in which the triadic relation of concepts-events-records is paramount.

Theory: Ausubel's assimilation theory of meaningful learning.

Novak's theory of conceptual education

Gowin's theory of educating

Principles:

1. In meaningful learning, new knowledge is subsumed by already existing cognitive structure elements.

2. The assimilation of new meaning transforms the meaning of both prior knowledge and newly acquired knowledge.

3. Cognitive structure develops by progressive differentiation and integrative reconciliation.

4. Cognitive structure is organized hierarchically according to levels of inclusiveness.

FOCUS QUESTIONS:

1. How do concept mapping and Gowin's Vee strategies influence a high school biology student in a school year's time?

2. What difference do these heuristic devices make to teacher and student in facilitating more meaningful learning and retention of knowledge in the high school biology class?

METHODOLOGICAL

Value claims:

1. A link between learning theory and teaching can be made by concept mapping and Vee instructional and learning strategies.

2. Their use in instruction and evaluation in biology is one valuable method.

Knowledge claims:

1. Student tapes suggest that learning strategies require *understanding* of the subject matter and are *hard work*, but also indicate that most students recognize and value understanding over rote learning.

2. Student concept map and test score improvement correlate significantly over time.

3. Student's concept map and test score improvement correlate significantly over time.

Transformations:

1. Student attitude change: *t* test

2. Test score improvement over time: scattergrams

3. Scattergrams of test scores correlated with concept map scores

4. Scattergrams of concept map scores over time

5. Pearson Correlation Coefficients of scattergrams

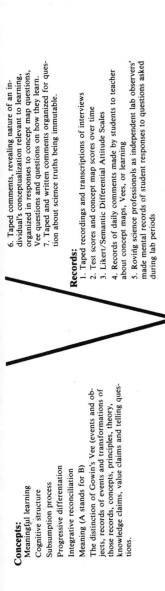

Concepts:
Meaningful learning
Cognitive structure
Subsumption process
Progressive differentiation
Integrative reconciliation
Meaning (A stands for B)
The distinction of Gowin's Vee (events and objects, records of events and transformations of those records, concepts, principles, theory, knowledge claims, value claims and telling questions.

6. Taped comments, revealing nature of an individual's conceptualization relevant to learning, organized in responses to concept map questions, Vee questions and questions on how they learn.
7. Taped and written comments organized for question about science truths being immutable.

Records:
1. Taped recordings and transcriptions of interviews
2. Test scores and concept map scores over time
3. Likert/Semantic Differential Attitude Scales
4. Records of daily comments made by students to teacher about concept maps, Vees, or learning
5. Roving science professionals as independent lab observers' made mental records of student responses to questions asked during lab periods

Objective/Events

Study of the performance on biology students who have concept maps and Vees

Study of taped interviews of students' responses to questions about how they learn and about concept mapping and Vees after 1-2 semesters and then again the following October

Figure 8.4 A Vee diagram for a study in high school biology classes that showed that students who used concept maps and Vee diagrams took more responsibility for learning than did traditionally instructed students (Gurley 1982).

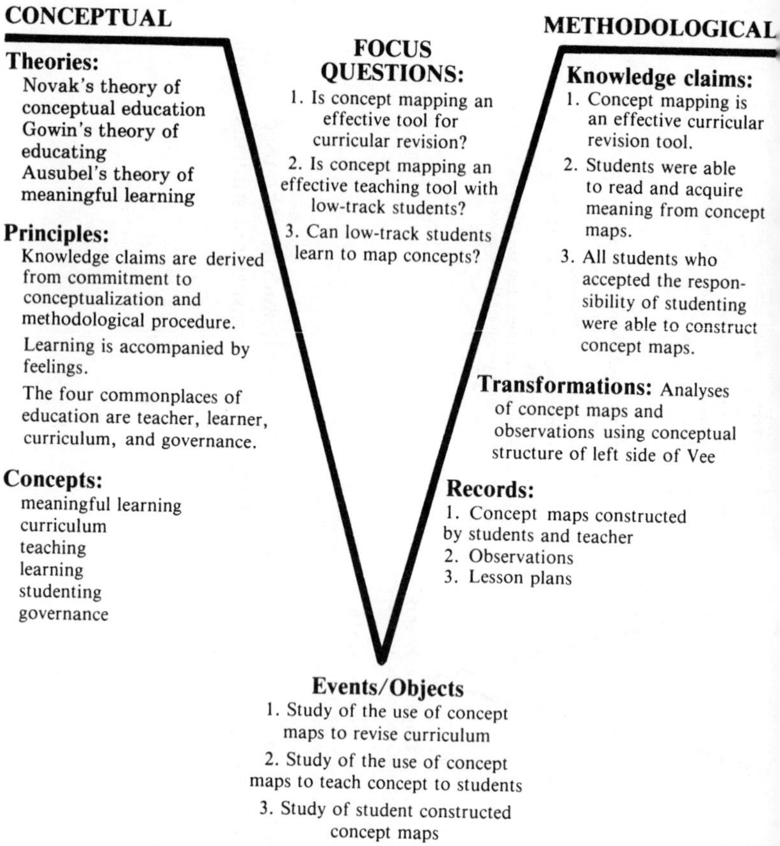

CONCEPTUAL

METHODOLOGICAL

Theories:
Novak's theory of
conceptual education
Gowin's theory of
educating
Ausubel's theory of
meaningful learning

Principles:
Knowledge claims are derived
from commitment to
conceptualization and
methodological procedure.

Learning is accompanied by
feelings.

The four commonplaces of
education are teacher, learner,
curriculum, and governance.

Concepts:
meaningful learning
curriculum
teaching
learning
studenting
governance

**FOCUS
QUESTIONS:**
1. Is concept mapping an
effective tool for
curricular revision?
2. Is concept mapping an
effective teaching tool with
low-track students?
3. Can low-track students
learn to map concepts?

Knowledge claims:
1. Concept mapping is
an effective curricular
revision tool.
2. Students were able
to read and acquire
meaning from concept
maps.
3. All students who
accepted the respon-
sibility of studenting
were able to construct
concept maps.

Transformations: Analyses
of concept maps and
observations using conceptual
structure of left side of Vee

Records:
1. Concept maps constructed
by students and teacher
2. Observations
3. Lesson plans

Events/Objects
1. Study of the use of concept
maps to revise curriculum
2. Study of the use of concept
maps to teach concept to students
3. Study of student constructed
concept maps

Figure 8.5 A study done with ninth-grade students on using concept mapping to modify the curriculum for low-achieving students (Melby-Robb 1982).

(5) Is it realistic to expect to gather these records in the time frame
we have planned and in the governance situation in which we
must work?

(6) Are the tests we have chosen *valid* measures of the phenomena in
the events we wish to observe? Will the measures produce facts?
How can we construct (or choose) a measure to evaluate the event
or outcomes we are intersted in?

(7) What kind of records are of particular concern (or interest) in
today's social-political environment?

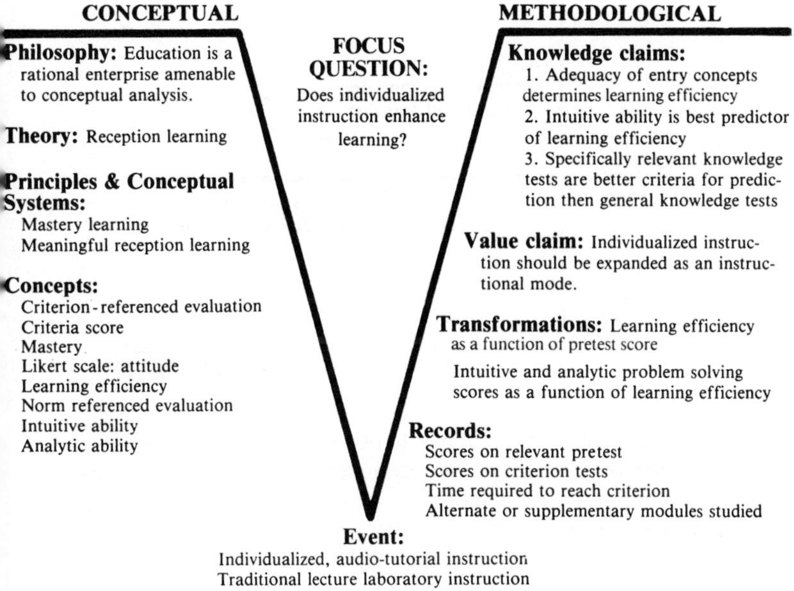

CONCEPTUAL	FOCUS QUESTION:	METHODOLOGICAL

Philosophy: Education is a rational enterprise amenable to conceptual analysis.

Theory: Reception learning

Principles & Conceptual Systems:
Mastery learning
Meaningful reception learning

Concepts:
Criterion-referenced evaluation
Criteria score
Mastery
Likert scale: attitude
Learning efficiency
Norm referenced evaluation
Intuitive ability
Analytic ability

FOCUS QUESTION:
Does individualized instruction enhance learning?

Knowledge claims:
1. Adequacy of entry concepts determines learning efficiency
2. Intuitive ability is best predictor of learning efficiency
3. Specifically relevant knowledge tests are better criteria for prediction then general knowledge tests

Value claim: Individualized instruction should be expanded as an instructional mode.

Transformations: Learning efficiency as a function of pretest score

Intuitive and analytic problem solving scores as a function of learning efficiency

Records:
Scores on relevant pretest
Scores on criterion tests
Time required to reach criterion
Alternate or supplementary modules studied

Event:
Individualized, audio-tutorial instruction
Traditional lecture laboratory instruction

Figure 8.6 A study comparing traditional lecture-laboratory with mastery mode audio-tutorial instruction in college physics. One of the findings of this study was that initial differences in knowledge of physics were compensated for in the audio-tutorial instructional format (Thorsland 1971).

(8) What kind of records do we believe have the most validity and reliability?

Record making is a crucial phase of any research study. Valid records are the raw facts from which we may construct valid claims. One of our critical concerns about meta-analysis[2] is that, as a statistical procedure for data transformation, it can mask poorly designed educative events, inadequate or invalid records of these events, or the lack of conceptual-theoretical ideas behind the construction of the events. Meta-analysis is not a method of data gathering but rather

2 Meta-analysis is a data-transforming technique developed recently that makes it possible to combine the results of a variety of research studies (see Glass, McGaw, and Smith 1981). Our concern is that if the records of the original studies were faulty, meta-analysis does not resolve the basic problem but can create an illusion of validity.

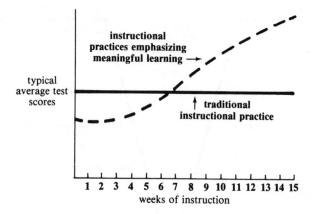

Figure 8.7 A graph of the commonly observed lowering of typical course examination score averages when meaningful learning strategies are required and later gains in score averages relative to those of groups receiving traditional instruction (see also Figure 8.8).

a method of data transformation, a difference that is overlooked in much current work.

In the last analysis, our knowledge claims can be no better or worse than the data-gathering tools we use. If the latter are faulty, no degree of elegant transformation will make them better. It is right at the bottom of the Vee, the record-making stage, that many educational research studies become useless. Poor records of educational events cannot lead to valid and reliable claims about those events. Even well-conceived studies that, unlike most educational research, succeed in conceptualizing significant events often fail to collect valid records.

RECORD TRANSFORMATION

Let us assume we have gathered valid records regarding the events or objects we have observed. The next step in the construction of knowledge is to seek regularities or patterns in these records. The primary purpose of transformations of records is to make discernible or more explicit salient regularities in our data. How do we proceed to choose the best tables, charts, graphs, models, or statistics to achieve effective transformations of the records? We must return to the left

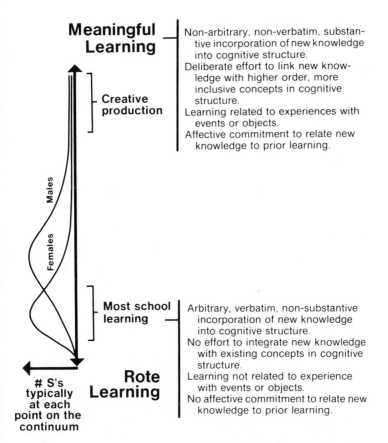

Meaningful Learning
Non-arbitrary, non-verbatim, substantive incorporation of new knowledge into cognitive structure.
Deliberate effort to link new knowledge with higher order, more inclusive concepts in cognitive structure.
Learning related to experiences with events or objects.
Affective commitment to relate new knowledge to prior learning.

Creative production

Males

Females

Most school learning
Arbitrary, verbatim, non-substantive incorporation of new knowledge into cognitive structure.
No effort to integrate new knowledge with existing concepts in cognitive structure.
Learning not related to experience with events or objects.
No affective commitment to relate new knowledge to prior learning.

S's typically at each point on the continuum

Rote Learning

Figure 8.8 A schematic representation of most school learning and creative production on the rote learning–meaningful learning continuum. Curves show relative differences between male and female populations' tendencies toward rote or meaningful learning (with differences exaggerated) (Ridley and Novak 1983).

side of the Vee and ask what concepts, principles, and theories are guiding the inquiry. These are the ideational elements that suggest how we might reasonably proceed in organizing the records we have. For example, if our guiding theory and principles say that sex and/or prior knowledge can influence learners' performance on a given task, then we should group the records of the learners' performance according to sex and levels of prior knowledge (recognizing that any

Table 8.1. *Categories chosen by one interviewee for food classification using cards illustrating foods*

Fruits	*Milk group*	*Combination dishes*
Grapefruit	Skim milk	Spaghetti
Peaches	Whole milk	Stew
Pear	Cream of tomato soup	Pizza
Meat	Milkshake	*Calories plus nonnutritive things*
Roast beef	*Bread/cereal*	
Liver	White bread	Gelatin
Bologna	Oatmeal	Sherbet
Vegetables	Cornflakes	Beer
Carrots	Whole wheat bread	Wine
Broccoli	Crackers	Coffee
Celery		Chicken noodle soup
Baked potato		Popcorn
		Butter
		Fat

test for the latter is only an estimate, always with some degree of bias). We might proceed to construct a table or a graph showing differences in performance by sex and/or by extent of prior knowledge.

Statistical methods can be useful for record transformation, but they are not a substitute for careful planning of the educational events to be observed or careful consideration of the validity of the record-making devices (usually paper-and-pencil tests) to be used. Whereas most books on educational research methods provide guidance on the types of statistical tests that can be employed, they rarely deal with the theoretical issues or with the highly constrained nature of test scores and the need for other kinds of records like those presented in this book. When statistical methods are carefully selected and interpreted, however, they can aid in controlling variables (through regression analysis or analysis of covariance) and in assigning probability values to various sources of numerical or categorical differences. As critical as some of our comments have been with regard to what we see as the abuse of statistical tools, we nevertheless recognize the importance and value of relevant statistics for data transformation.

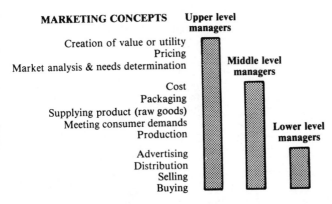

Figure 8.9 Simple graphic data transformation illustrating interview findings that middle and/or upper level managers operate with concepts not held by lower level managers.

Wherever it is appropriate, we favor use of the simplest forms of data transformation. This keeps our claims close to the original events or objects observed and close to the raw records we have made. The less complicated the methodological path from events or objects to claims, the more likely we are to have confidence in the validity of our claims, and the easier it will be to apply our claims to the design of new and better educational events.

Table 8.1 shows a simple translation of data obtained in an event where subjects were asked to explain their groupings and the nutritional significance of those groupings. The results for one individual, shown in Table 8.1, indicate that this person has a good set of concepts regarding nutritional value of common foods (though of course coffee has no caloric value unless sugar and cream are added). Figure 8.9 shows another example of relatively simple data transformations from interviews, where management concepts were grouped according to the level of the manager expressing them, from those typically given by lower level managers (e.g., a store hardware department manager) to those given by upper level managers (e.g., director of marketing for a large corporation). Because upper level managers presumably also have knowledge of the concepts held by lower level managers, one could speculate on how or why people at different levels in the management hierarchy shared different frameworks of concepts. A concept map drawn from an interview with a professor

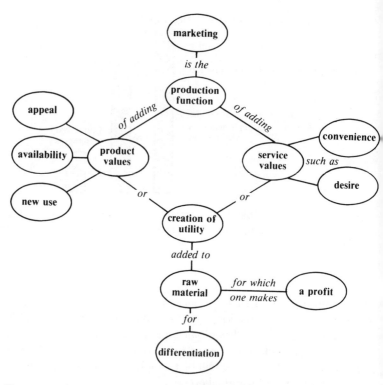

Figure 8.10 A concept map prepared from an interview with a Cornell University professor of marketing showing his higher order marketing concepts and a well-integrated conceptual framework (Geri Gay, personal communication).

of marketing at Cornell University (Figure 8.10) shows the most comprehensive hierarchical set of concepts. Concept maps and videotaped interviews from the project that produced these data have been used in management training programs at Cornell.

It is also important to construct summary data statistics in such a way as to illustrate clear relationships between the theory or principles guiding the inquiry and the resultant data. Research in the Piagetian model has been so well accepted in education in recent years because both the kinds of data gathered and the type of data transformations (emphasizing individual rather than group performance) so nicely follow from the events in Piagetian interviews.

Nevertheless, we should recognize the very restricted range of events to which Piagetian theory is relevant. By contrast, Ausubelian cognitive learning theory applies to the full range of cognitive school learning tasks (Novak 1977b, 1979, Modgil and Modgil 1982). Many theories can be constructed to explain a narrow set of events; what is needed are theories that are simple in their explanatory principles and yet are relevant to a wide range of events (Novak 1977a).

KNOWLEDGE CLAIMS

Finally, we reach the point in any productive inquiry where we construct knowledge claims. We cannot say this or that is true; what we can say is that, based on the educational events observed, the kind of data collected, and our data transformations, our knowledge claims are valid, and that we recognize that a different structure of educational events and/or the collection of different data or the use of alternative data transformation procedures may have led to different (perhaps in some cases diametrically opposing) knowledge claims. In addition, the whole inquiry must be consistent, with each aspect of our research Vee structure logically related to every other aspect, and/or justified on previous empirical grounds. Only in this way can we hope to progress in our understanding of educational events and in the knowledge that will permit us to design better educational events in the future.

The same epistemological necessities operate in any of the four commonplaces: teaching, learning, curriculum, or governance. The claims we must seek to make in each of these four domains of educating must derive from the same kind of clear relationship between conceptual-theoretical principles and methodological procedures. The nature of the questions we construct, the type of events we choose (or construct) to observe, and the data and data transformations can vary, but all should be guided by our conceptual-theoretical ideas of education.

Reporting results may therefore be anything but simple. First, we must be sure that proper reference is made to the theoretical ideas guiding our inquiry. Programmatic research makes reporting easier because statements on the theoretical basis of the work have usually already been published (although with some studies, such as those in the Piagetian tradition, so many and such diverse statements are published that it is difficult to say explicitly what the theory is). The senior investigator has the obligation to state as explicitly as possible the guiding theory behind an inquiry (see for example Bloom 1976, Novak 1977a, or Gowin 1981). This is not to say that the theory is "frozen"; any useful theory will continue to evolve, and to be amended and extended.

Second, we must be as explicit as possible in describing the educational events we have constructed, and in relating that description to the theoretical framework that guided the inquiry. This can be a challenge. Some experiments may have an unusually complex set of specially constructed events (for example, our "learning how to learn" project [Novak and staff 1981]) that may take a book-length report to describe. Once again, there is an advantage to programmatic research in that the senior researcher may already have published a general description of the educational events and data-gathering methodologies.

Third, it is important to explain the concepts and theories that guided the data collection and/or data transformation. This aspect is too often ignored or omitted in educational research reports. (Of course, as too often happens, if no concepts or theories guided the inquiry, then there is nothing to report.) We may assume that it is self-evident that data of type X or data transformation procedure Y should have been used. To the critical educational researcher, however, particularly one who is operating from a different conceptual-theoretical framework, the type of data we collected or the type of data transformations we used are not at all self-evident! (We cannot make claims regarding meaningful learning, for example, if our data deal only with test results for rote recall of facts.) Furthermore, in trying to justify to others the kind of data or transformation we used to make our knowledge claims, we often see new alternatives that can be more productive. It is then that our "recommendations for future research" are truly useful, and not simply banal recommendations for "more of the same."

Finally, research is knowledge production. No one should know better than the researcher the strengths and weaknesses of the knowledge claims produced, and good research reports should spell out those strengths and weaknesses of the inquiry and not assume that the data speak for themselves, which is never completely the case. Our claims must be checked against the data we have collected: In our best judgment, do the data truly support each of the claims we seek to make?

VALUE CLAIMS

If we believe our research has produced something of significance, something that has social value, our reports should state our value claims as well as our knowledge claims. We should, of course, be explicit in making a distinction between the two types of claims. Value claims usually derive from knowledge claims but they are not the same thing. For example, one can make a knowledge claim that it can be demonstrated that the use of learning heuristics enhances cognitive learning, but to conclude that the use of these heuristics should be increased in schools is a value claim.

Value claims are answers to value questions (Gowin and Green 1980, Gowin 1981). We have found that there are five kinds of value questions. *Instrumental* value claims take the form, Is X good for Y? For example, is metalearning instruction with concept maps good for acquisition and retention of knowledge? *Intrinsic* value claims take the form, Is X good? or, Is X something society values? For example, is there intrinsic worth in helping students learn more about how they learn? *Comparative* value claims take the form, Is X better than Y? For example, is time spent on learning concept mapping better used than time spent on learning additional subject matter? *Decision* value claims take the form, Is X right? or, Ought we to choose X? Here we deal with judgments such as, Even if it can be demonstrated empirically that metalearning and/or metaknowledge strategies facilitate, for example, long-term transfer of knowledge in problem solving, is it right to teach students these strategies? Finally, *idealized* value claims take the form, Is X as good as it can be, or can it be made better? For example, is Vee diagramming, as we now employ it, a good metaknowledge strategy, or can we improve on it?

Value questions are not the same as knowledge questions, but the answers to them are clearly related to the answers to knowledge questions. Furthermore, the value questions are related to one another. For example, if encouragement of meaningful learning (as opposed to rote learning) was not considered socially desirable then this decision value claim would take precedence over an intrinsic value claim that concept mapping is good for encouraging meaningful learning. Asking if concept mapping is the best strategy (or are there better ones?) is a comparative value question. And if there were some question about the intrinsic value of concept mapping as it is now used, we would ask how our methods of teaching and using this strategy could be improved – a question of idealized value.

Classical empiricist and positivist philosophies denied that value questions and value claims had a legitimate place in a rational enterprise of knowledge construction. Contemporary philosophies, on the other hand, see value questions as crucial to the advance of our understanding in any discipline. Obviously, we hold the latter view.

CONCLUSION

We conclude that educational research can produce impressive results in the coming decades. We summarize with a few simple "dos and don'ts" for researchers:

(1) Organize or join programmatic research efforts that have an explicit framework of guiding theories and concepts.
(2) Be innovative in creating educational events, gathering records, and transforming or reporting data.
(3) Be explicit in showing how the guiding theory and concepts relate to the events constructed and the data organized. Use the Vee.
(4) Show not only how knowledge claims derive from the events and data, but also how they relate to the conceptual-theoretical framework.
(5) Do not confuse value claims. Although the data regarding the success of an alternative learning procedure may be persuasive, the value of any procedure is also dependent upon its costs, on human sensitivities and goals, and on other social issues.
(6) Do not assume that there is only one set of valid claims that could be derived from the events and record constructed. Keep alert for better, alternative ways to view these events and/or data.
(7) Recognize that knowledge that increases human understanding is constructed, that claims from any one inquiry are just a brick or two in the construction of knowledge about educating, and that some of this knowledge will be cast aside in later inquiries.
(8) Report claims. Research left unpublished is not likely to contribute much.
(9) Keep on researching! Societies can and will benefit from better and expanded educational research (a value claim!).

APPENDIXES

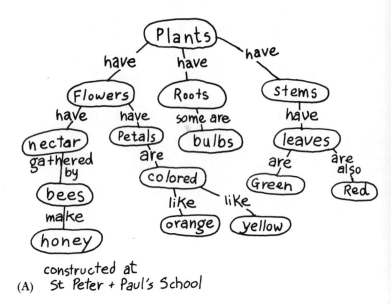

(A) constructed at St Peter + Paul's School

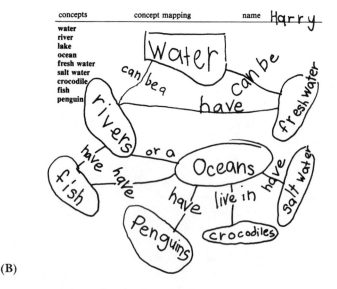

(B)

Figure I.1 A concept map **(A)** constructed with a first-grade class to illustrate how to make concept maps. A week later, children were given sheets with lists of words previously discussed in class and each constructed their own

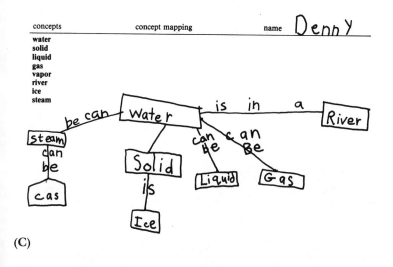

(C)

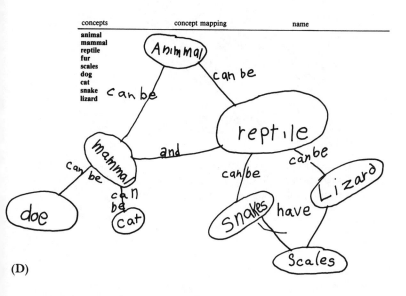

(D)

concept map. Representative maps (**B, C,** and **D**) show keen awareness of concept meanings although Denny (Map **C**) either omitted or did not know the meaning relationship for *vapor*.

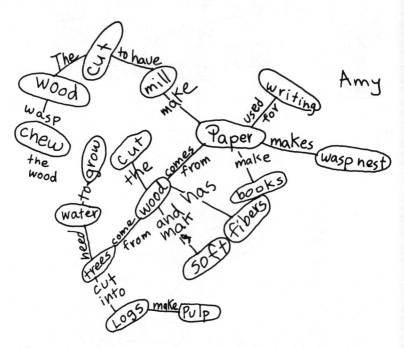

Figure I.2 A concept map constructed by a fourth-grade student, following a field trip to a paper mill, showing a good integration of concept meanings (see also Figure 5.5 showing poor integration of meanings).

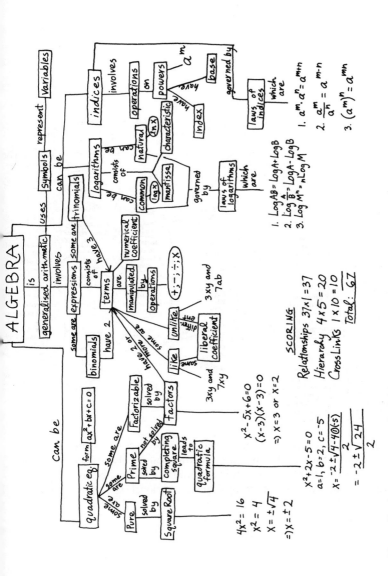

Figure I.3 A concept map for high school algebra constructed for a math review course for black African students (John Volmink, personal communication).

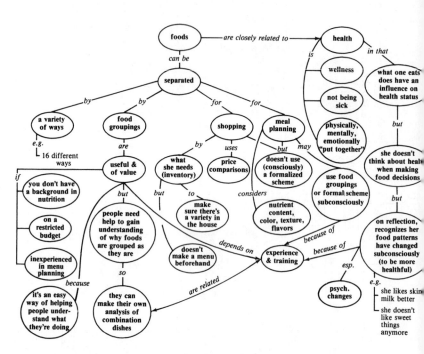

Figure I.4 A concept map constructed by a student from an interview transcript on nutrition. This map shows a common problem observed in that sets of concept are included in ovals. Students need to be encouraged to separate out such concept sets by forming additional concept networks.

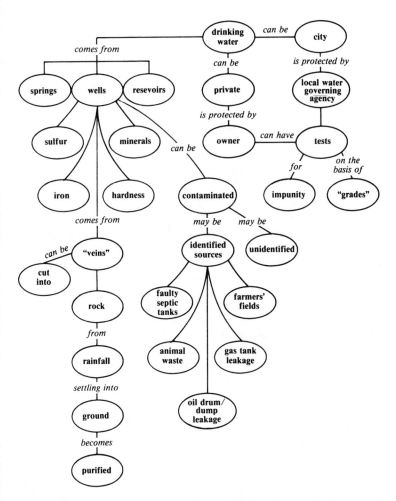

Figure I.5 A concept map prepared to guide interviews with the general public regarding their understanding of the origins of drinking water.

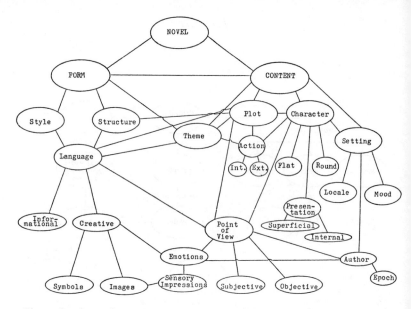

Figure I.6 An early concept map constructed by Marli Moreira (1977) as a basis for organizing instruction in literature. Lines connecting concepts were not labeled in our earlier work.

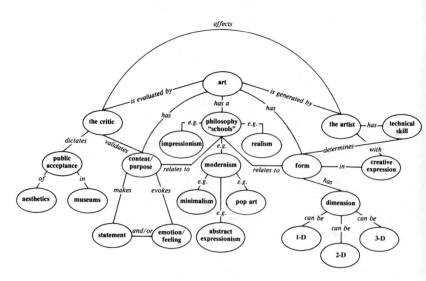

Figure I.7 A concept map prepared to guide interviews regarding individuals' understanding of art.

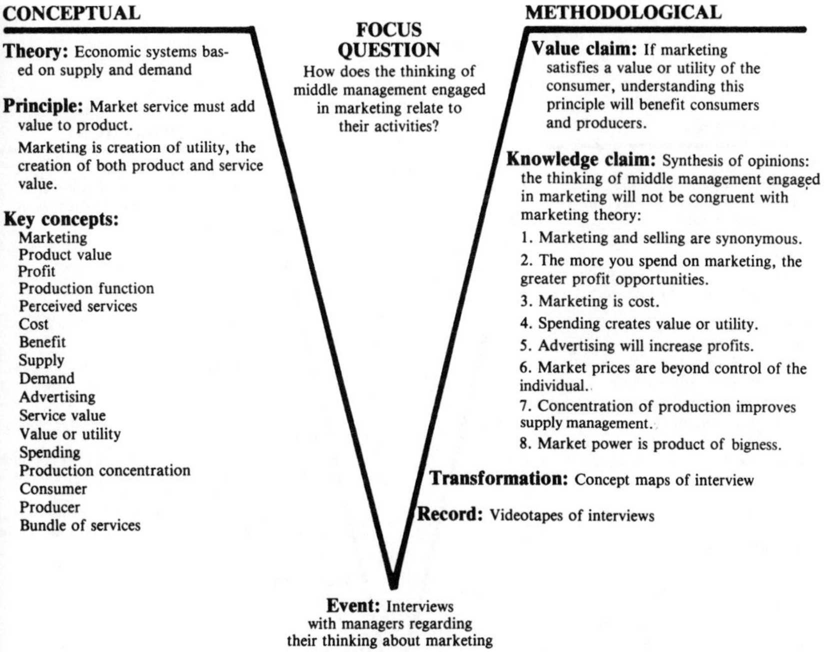

CONCEPTUAL

FOCUS QUESTION
How does the thinking of middle management engaged in marketing relate to their activities?

METHODOLOGICAL

Theory: Economic systems based on supply and demand

Principle: Market service must add value to product.

Marketing is creation of utility, the creation of both product and service value.

Key concepts:
Marketing
Product value
Profit
Production function
Perceived services
Cost
Benefit
Supply
Demand
Advertising
Service value
Value or utility
Spending
Production concentration
Consumer
Producer
Bundle of services

Value claim: If marketing satisfies a value or utility of the consumer, understanding this principle will benefit consumers and producers.

Knowledge claim: Synthesis of opinions: the thinking of middle management engaged in marketing will not be congruent with marketing theory:

1. Marketing and selling are synonymous.

2. The more you spend on marketing, the greater profit opportunities.

3. Marketing is cost.

4. Spending creates value or utility.

5. Advertising will increase profits.

6. Market prices are beyond control of the individual.

7. Concentration of production improves supply management.

8. Market power is product of bigness.

Transformation: Concept maps of interview

Record: Videotapes of interviews

Event: Interviews with managers regarding their thinking about marketing

Figure II.1 A Vee map constructed to guide an inquiry on the concepts held by persons at various levels of management (see also Figures 8.9 and 8.10).

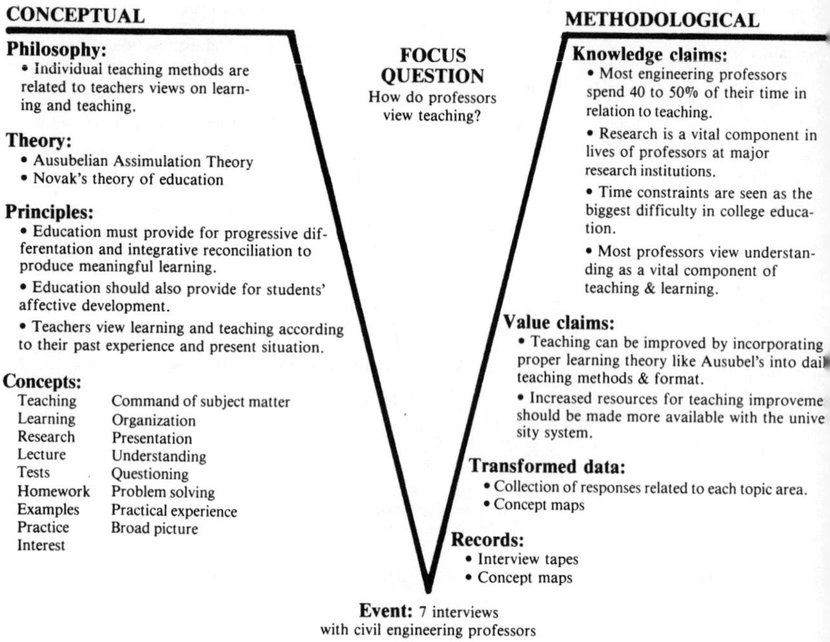

CONCEPTUAL

METHODOLOGICAL

FOCUS QUESTION

How do professors view teaching?

Philosophy:
• Individual teaching methods are related to teachers views on learning and teaching.

Theory:
• Ausubelian Assimilation Theory
• Novak's theory of education

Principles:
• Education must provide for progressive differentation and integrative reconciliation to produce meaningful learning.
• Education should also provide for students' affective development.
• Teachers view learning and teaching according to their past experience and present situation.

Concepts:

Teaching	Command of subject matter
Learning	Organization
Research	Presentation
Lecture	Understanding
Tests	Questioning
Homework	Problem solving
Examples	Practical experience
Practice	Broad picture
Interest	

Knowledge claims:
• Most engineering professors spend 40 to 50% of their time in relation to teaching.
• Research is a vital component in lives of professors at major research institutions.
• Time constraints are seen as the biggest difficulty in college education.
• Most professors view understanding as a vital component of teaching & learning.

Value claims:
• Teaching can be improved by incorporating proper learning theory like Ausubel's into daily teaching methods & format.
• Increased resources for teaching improvement should be made more available with the university system.

Transformed data:
• Collection of responses related to each topic area.
• Concept maps

Records:
• Interview tapes
• Concept maps

Event: 7 interviews with civil engineering professors

Figure II.2 A Vee map constructed to guide a student's inquiry into professors' views of teaching.

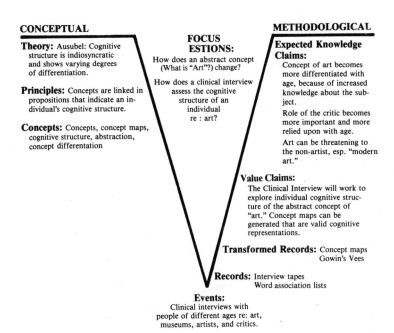

CONCEPTUAL

Theory: Ausubel: Cognitive structure is indiosyncratic and shows varying degrees of differentiation.

Principles: Concepts are linked in propositions that indicate an individual's cognitive structure.

Concepts: Concepts, concept maps, cognitive structure, abstraction, concept differentiation

FOCUS ESTIONS:

How does an abstract concept (What is "Art"?) change?

How does a clinical interview assess the cognitive structure of an individual re : art?

METHODOLOGICAL

Expected Knowledge Claims:
Concept of art becomes more differentiated with age, because of increased knowledge about the subject.

Role of the critic becomes more important and more relied upon with age.

Art can be threatening to the non-artist, esp. "modern art."

Value Claims:
The Clinical Interview will work to explore individual cognitive structure of the abstract concept of "art." Concept maps can be generated that are valid cognitive representations.

Transformed Records: Concept maps
Gowin's Vees

Records: Interview tapes
Word association lists

Events:
Clinical interviews with people of different ages re: art, museums, artists, and critics.

Figure II.3 A Vee map prepared to guide an inquiry into persons' concepts of art (see also Figure I.7).

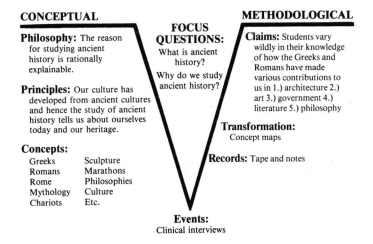

CONCEPTUAL

Philosophy: The reason for studying ancient history is rationally explainable.

Principles: Our culture has developed from ancient cultures and hence the study of ancient history tells us about ourselves today and our heritage.

Concepts:

Greeks	Sculpture
Romans	Marathons
Rome	Philosophies
Mythology	Culture
Chariots	Etc.

FOCUS QUESTIONS:
What is ancient history?

Why do we study ancient history?

METHODOLOGICAL

Claims: Students vary wildly in their knowledge of how the Greeks and Romans have made various contributions to us in 1.) architecture 2.) art 3.) government 4.) literature 5.) philosophy

Transformation:
Concept maps

Records: Tape and notes

Events:
Clinical interviews

Figure II.4 A Vee map constructed to study college students' concepts of ancient history.

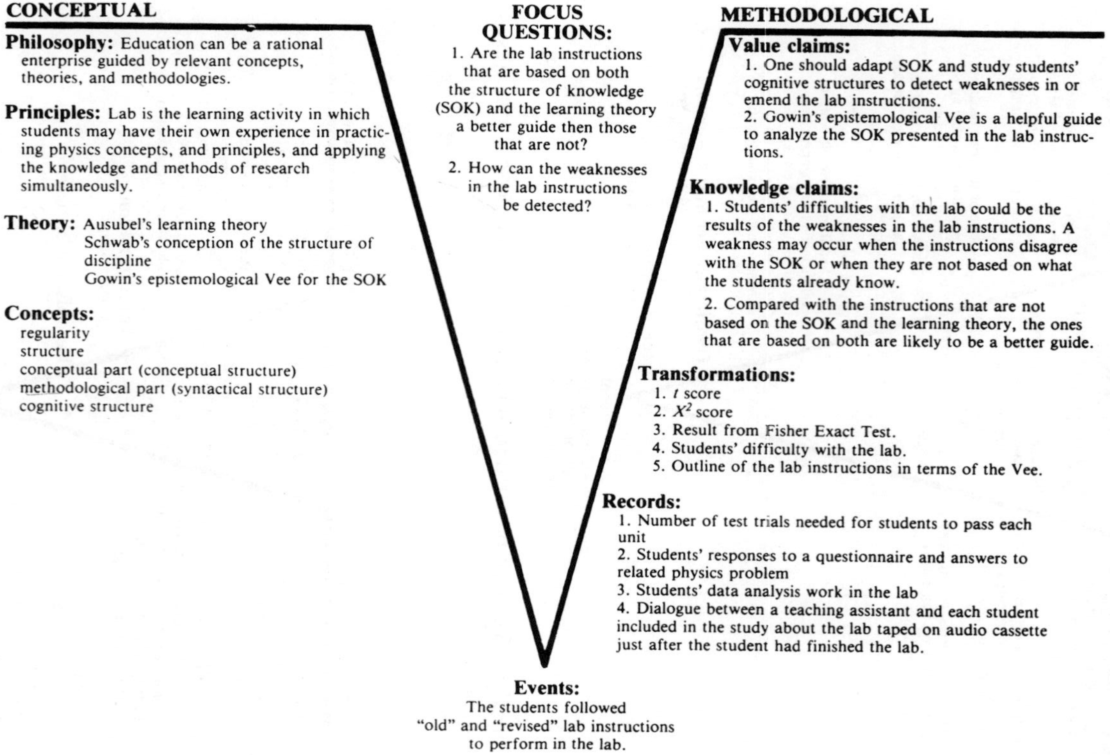

CONCEPTUAL

Philosophy: Education can be a rational enterprise guided by relevant concepts, theories, and methodologies.

Principles: Lab is the learning activity in which students may have their own experience in practicing physics concepts, and principles, and applying the knowledge and methods of research simultaneously.

Theory: Ausubel's learning theory
Schwab's conception of the structure of discipline
Gowin's epistemological Vee for the SOK

Concepts:
regularity
structure
conceptual part (conceptual structure)
methodological part (syntactical structure)
cognitive structure

FOCUS QUESTIONS:

1. Are the lab instructions that are based on both the structure of knowledge (SOK) and the learning theory a better guide then those that are not?

2. How can the weaknesses in the lab instructions be detected?

METHODOLOGICAL

Value claims:

1. One should adapt SOK and study students' cognitive structures to detect weaknesses in or emend the lab instructions.

2. Gowin's epistemological Vee is a helpful guide to analyze the SOK presented in the lab instructions.

Knowledge claims:

1. Students' difficulties with the lab could be the results of the weaknesses in the lab instructions. A weakness may occur when the instructions disagree with the SOK or when they are not based on what the students already know.

2. Compared with the instructions that are not based on the SOK and the learning theory, the ones that are based on both are likely to be a better guide.

Transformations:
1. t score
2. X^2 score
3. Result from Fisher Exact Test.
4. Students' difficulty with the lab.
5. Outline of the lab instructions in terms of the Vee.

Records:
1. Number of test trials needed for students to pass each unit
2. Students' responses to a questionnaire and answers to related physics problem
3. Students' data analysis work in the lab
4. Dialogue between a teaching assistant and each student included in the study about the lab taped on audio cassette just after the student had finished the lab.

Events:
The students followed "old" and "revised" lab instructions to perform in the lab.

Figure II.5 A Vee map representing Chen's (1980) Master's thesis research (see also Figure 4.5).

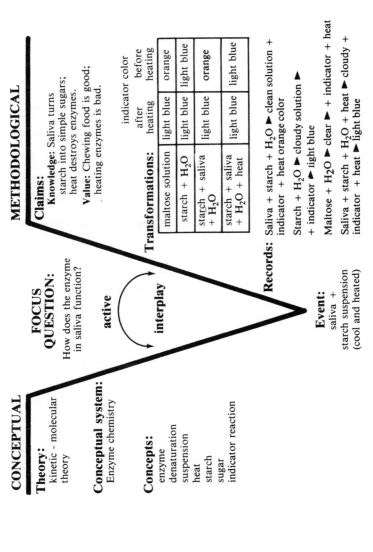

Figure II.6 A Vee map constructed with a seventh grade biology class from a laboratory investigation on enzyme function.

Ithaca City School District
Ithaca, New York

Dear Parent:

From time to time we are called upon by Cornell University, Ithaca College, or some other agency interested in the education of young people, to participate cooperatively in research activity involving students attending the Ithaca public schools. In keeping with Board of Education policy only those students whose parents or guardians have given permission will be allowed to participate in such projects.

Your child, _____, is being considered for participation in a research project being conducted by _____ _____. The purpose of this study is _____. Your child will be asked _____ _____.

If for some reason you <u>do not want</u> your child to participate in this study please notify me or the school principal by signing this letter.

_____
Principal

_____
Researcher   Phone No.

Figure III.1 Sample letter to parents requesting permission for their child to participate in a research project.

188

Appendixes

APPLICATION FOR RESEARCH PRIVILEGES
Ithaca City School District
Ithaca, New York

Date _____ , 19 _____

DIRECTIONS:

1. Discuss your project with your college/department representative, if appropriate.
2. Complete 5 copies of this application.
3. Attach approval of University Committee on Human Subjects.
4. Send 4 copies signed by the University Committee on Human Subjects to the office of CALS Department of Education Research Coordinator (256-6515 - Stone).
5. The Department of Education Research Coordinator will forward 2 copies of your application to the Ithaca Public School District and return 1 signed copy to you.

Name of applicant _____ Home Phone _____

Mailing Address _____ Cornell Phone _____

GENERAL INFORMATION:

1. Title of project _____
2. Purpose _____
   _____
3. Research instruments or procedures: Attach full outline of Project and a copy of instruments.
4. Desired Dates: Begin _____ 19___ . End _____ 19 ___ .
5. Pupil Involvement Requested: Age or grade level _____ .
6. Time requested: a) Individual sessions: Number of pupils _____ ; Number of sessions per pupil _____ ; Length of time per pupil per session _____ ; Total time spent with individuals _____ .
   b) Class or Group Sessions: Size of group _____ ; Number of groups _____ ; Number of sessions per group _____ ; Length of time per session _____ ; Total number of pupil hours _____ .
7. Teacher Involvement Requested _____

SPONSORSHIP:
1. Professor directing the research _____ Department _____
2. Project title or source of funding _____
3. Other participating personnel from Cornell _____

PARTICIPANTS FROM THE ITHACA CITY SCHOOL DISTRICT:
1. Ithaca schools whose classes are to be used:

   School _____ Grade(s) _____ No. of Pupils _____ Teacher(s) _____
   School _____ Grade(s) _____ No. of Pupils _____ Teacher(s) _____
   School _____ Grade(s) _____ No. of Pupils _____ Teacher(s) _____

APPROVAL (required in order listed below)

1. _____   4. _____
   Committee on Human Subjects   Director, Pupil Personnel

2. _____   5. _____
   Department of Education Research   Assistant Superintendent
   Coordinator

3. _____
   Building Principal(s)

Figure III.2 Sample of a form for application for research privileges.

REFERENCES

Ault, C. R., J. D. Novak, and D. B. Gowin. In press. "Using the Knowledge Vee to Interpret Clinical Interview Data: A New Methodology." *Science Education.*

Ausubel, David P. 1963. *The Psychology of Meaningful Verbal Learning.* New York: Grune & Stratton.

___. 1968. *Educational Psychology: A Cognitive View.* New York: Holt, Rinehart and Winston.

Ausubel, David P., J. D. Novak, and H. Hanesian. 1978. *Educational Psychology: A Cognitive View,* 2nd ed. New York: Holt, Rinehart and Winston.

Benbow, C. P., and J. C. Stanley. 1982. "Consequences in High School and College of Sex Differences in Mathematical Reasoning Ability: A Longitudinal Perspective." *American Educational Research Journal,* 14: 15–71.

___. 1983. "Sex Differences in Mathematical Ability: More facts." *Science,* 222:1029–31.

Bloom, Benjamin S. 1956. *Taxonomy of Educational Objectives: The Classification of Educational Goals, Handbook I: Cognitive Domain.* New York: McKay.

___. 1968. "Learning for Mastery." *UCLA Evaluation Comment,* 1(2): 1.

___. 1976. *Human Characteristics and School Learning.* New York: McGraw-Hill.

Bogden, Christopher A. 1977. "The Use of Concept Mapping as a Possible Strategy for Instructional Design and Evaluation in College Genetics." Master's thesis, Cornell University.

Brown, H. I. 1979. *Perception, Theory and Commitment: The New Philosophy of Science,* Phoenix ed. Chicago: University of Chicago Press.

Buchweitz, Bernardo. 1981. "An Epistemological Analysis of Curriculum and an Assessment of Concept Learning in the Physics Laboratory." PhD thesis, Cornell University.

Cardemone, Peter F. 1975. "Concept Mapping: A Technique of Analyzing a Discipline and its Use in the Curriculum and Instruction in a Portion

References

of a College Level Mathematics Skills Course." Master's thesis, Cornell University.

Chen, Hai Hsia. 1980. "Relevance of Gowin's Structure of Knowledge and Ausubel's Learning Theory to Methods for Improving Physics Laboratory Instruction." Master's thesis, Cornell University.

Clement, John. "Students' Preconceptions in Introductory Mechanics." *American Journal of Physics,* 50(1): 66–71.

Conant, James B. 1947. *On Understanding Science.* New Haven: Yale University Press.

Donaldson, Margaret. 1978. *Children's Minds.* London: Fontana.

Easley, J. A. 1974. "The Structural Paradigm in Protocol Analysis." *Journal of Research in Science Teaching,* 11: 281–90.

Ebbinghaus, Hermann. 1913. *Memory: A Contribution to Experimental Psychology.* Henry G. Ruger, transl. New York: Teachers College Press.

Fennema, E., and J. Sherman. 1977. "Sex-Related Differences in Mathematics Achievement, Spatial Visualization and Affective Factors." *American Educational Research Journal,* 19:598–622.

Ghiselin, Brewster. 1952. *The Creative Process.* Berkeley: University of California Press.

Gilligan, Carol. 1982. *In a Different Voice: Psychological Theory and Women's Development.* Cambridge, Mass.: Harvard University Press.

Glass, G. V., B. V. McGaw, and M. L. Smith. 1981. *Meta-analysis in Social Research.* Beverley Hills, Calif.: Sage.

Goodnight, Clarence J., Marie L. Goodnight, and Peter Gray. 1964. *General Zoology.* New York: Van Nostrand Reinhold.

Gould, Stephen Jay. 1981. *The Mismeasure of Man.* New York: Norton.

Gowin, D. Bob. 1970. "The Structure of Knowledge." *Educational Theory,* 20(4): 319–28.

——— 1972. "Is Educational Research Distinctive?" In L. G. Thomas (ed.), *Philosophical Redirection of Educational Research,* 71st Yearbook of the National Society for the Study of Education, part 1, pp. 9–25.

——— 1981. *Educating.* Ithaca, N.Y.: Cornell University Press.

——— 1982. "Philosophy of Science in Education." In H. E. Mitzel (ed.), *Encyclopedia of Educational Research,* 5th ed., vol. 3. New York: Free Press, pp. 1413–16.

Gowin, D. Bob, and Thomas Green. 1980. *The Evaluation Document: Philosophic Structure.* Portland, Ore.: Northwest Regional Educational Laboratory, Publication No. 30.

Gunstone, Richard F., and Richard T. White. 1981. "Understanding of Gravity." *Science Education,* 65(3): 291–9.

Gurley, 'Laine I. 1982. "Use of Gowin's Vee and Concept Mapping Strategies to Teach Responsibility for Learning in High School Biological Sciences." PhD thesis, Cornell University.

References

Harris, Thomas A. 1967. *I'm OK – You're OK*. New York: Harper & Row.

Herrigel, E. 1973. *Zen in the Art of Archery*. New York: Random House.

Hoffman, Banesh. 1962. *The Tyranny of Testing*. New York: Crowell-Collier.

Holt, John. 1964. *How Children Fail*. New York: Pitman.

Johnson, Mauritz, Jr. 1967. "Definitions and Models in Curriculum Theory." *Educational Theory*, 17(2): 127–40.

Joyce James. 1946. *Eveline, a novel*. In Silberboot Almanach, Salzburg.

Keil, Frank C. 1979. *Semantic and Conceptual Development: An Ontological Perspective*. Cambridge, Mass.: Harvard University Press.

Kinigstein, June B. 1981. "A Conceptual Approach to Planning and Environmental Education Curriculum." Master's thesis, Cornell University.

Kohlberg, L. 1964. "Development of Moral Character and Moral Ideology." *Review of Child Development Research*, 1: 383–431.

Kuhn, Thomas S. 1962. *The Structure of Scientific Revolutions*. In *International Encyclopedia of Unified Sciences*, 2nd ed. Chicago: University of Chicago Press.

Loehr, Raymond C., William J. Jewell, Joseph D. Novak, William W. Clarkson, and Gerald S. Friedman. 1979. *Land Application of Wastes*, vols. 1 and 2. New York: Van Nostrand Reinhold.

Macnamara, John. 1982. *Names for Things: A Study of Human Learning*. Cambridge, Mass.: M.I.T. Press.

Melby-Robb, Susan J. 1982. "An Exploration of the Uses of Concept Mapping with Science Students Labeled Low Achievers." Master's thesis, Cornell University.

Miller, George A. 1956. "The Magical Number Seven, Plus or Minus Two: Some Limits on our Capacity for Processing Information." *Psychological Review*, 63: 81–97.

Minemier, Leah. 1983. "Concept Mapping: An Educational Tool and its Use in a College Level Mathematics Skills Course." Master's thesis, Cornell University.

Modgil, Sohan, and Celia Modgil. 1982. *Jean Piaget: Consensus and Controversy*. New York: Praeger.

Moreira, Marco A. 1977. "An Ausubelian Approach to Physics Instruction: An Experiment in an Introductory College Course in Electromagnetism." PhD thesis, Cornell University.

———. 1979. "Concept Maps as Tools for Teaching." *Journal of College Science Teaching*, 8(5): 283–6.

Novak, Joseph D. 1977a. *A Theory of Education*. Ithaca, N.Y.: Cornell University Press.

———. 1977b. "An Alternative to Piagetian Psychology for Science and Mathematics Education." *Science Education*, 61(4): 453–77.

———. 1979a. "Applying Psychology and Philosophy to the Improvement of Laboratory Teaching." *American Biology Teacher*, 41(8): 466–70.

References

1979b. "The Reception Learning Paradigm." *Journal of Research in Science Teaching,* 16(6): 481–8.

1980. "Learning Theory Applied to the Biology Classroom." *American Biology Teacher,* 42(5): 280–5.

1981. "Applying Learning Psychology and Philosophy of Science to Biology Teaching." *American Biology Teacher,* 43 (1): 10–12.

1982. "A Need for Caution in the Use of Research Claims to Guide Biology Teaching." *American Biology Teacher,* 44(7): 393.

In press. "Metalearning and Metaknowledge Strategies to Help Students Learn How to Learn." In A. L. Pines and L. H. T. West (eds.), *Cognitive Structure and Conceptual Change.* New York: Academic Press.

Novak, Joseph D., and D. Bob Gowin. 1981. "Concept Mapping and Other Innovative Strategies." Unpublished manuscript, Cornell University.

Novak, Joseph D., D. Bob Gowin, and Gerard T. Johansen. 1983. "The Use of Concept Mapping and Knowledge Vee Mapping with Junior High School Science Students." *Science Education,* 67(5): 625–45.

Novak, Joseph D., and staff. 1981. "The Use of Concept Mapping and Gowin's Vee Mapping Instructional Strategies in Junior High School Science." Unpublished report on NSF project (SED 78-16762), Cornell University.

Novak, Joseph D., and David Symington. 1982. "Concept Mapping for Curriculum Development." *Victoria Institute of Educational Research Bulletin,* 48: 3–11.

Novick, Shimson, and Joseph Nussbaum. 1978. "Junior High School Pupils' Understanding of the Particulate Nature of Matter: An Interview Study." *Science Education,* 62(3): 273–81.

Nussbaum, Joseph. 1983. "Classroom Conceptual Change: The Lesson to Be Learned from the History of Science." In Hugh Helm and Joseph D. Novak (eds.), *Proceedings of the International Seminar on Misconceptions in Science and Mathematics.* Ithaca, N.Y.: Department of Education, Cornell University; pp. 272–81.

Nussbaum, Joseph, and Joseph D. Novak. 1976. "An Assessment of Children's Concepts of the Earth Utilizing Structured Interviews." *Science Education,* 60(4): 535–50.

Oram, Raymond, Paul Hummer, and Robert Smoot. 1979. *Biology: Living Systems.* Columbus, Ohio: Merrill.

Page, Louise, and Esther Phipard. 1957. "Essentials of an Adequate Diet: Facts for Nutrition Programs." U.S. Department of Agriculture, Research Report No. 3.

Perry, William G., Jr. 1970. *Forms of Intellectual and Ethical Development in the College Years.* New York: Holt, Rinehart, and Winston.

Piaget, Jean. 1926. *The Language and Thought of the Child.* New York: Har-

References

court Brace.

Pines, Ariel Leon. 1977. "Scientific Concept Learning in Children: The Effect of Prior Knowledge on Resulting Cognitive Structure Subsequent to A–T Instruction." PhD thesis, Cornell University.

Postlethwait, S. N., J. D. Novak, and H. T. Murray, Jr. 1972. *The Audio-tutorial Approach to Learning*, 3rd ed. Minneapolis, Minn.: Burgess.

Ridley, Dennis R., and Joseph D. Novak. 1983. "Sex-related Differences in High School Science and Mathematics Enrollments: Do They Give Males a Critical Headstart Toward Science- and Math-related Careers?" *Alberta Journal of Educational Research*, 29(4): 308–18.

Ripple, R. E., and V. N. Rockcastle (eds.). 1964. Piaget Rediscovered: Selected Papers from a Report of the Conference on Cognitive Studies and Curriculum Development, March, 1964. *Journal of Research in Science Teaching*, 2(3): 165–267.

Rodgers, Joann E. 1982. "The Malleable Memory of Eyewitnesses." *Science 82*, 3(5): 32–5.

Rorty, Richard. 1979. *Philosophy and the Mirror of Nature*. Princeton: Princeton University Press.

Rowe, Mary B. 1974a. "Wait-time and Rewards as Instructional Variables: Their Influence on Learning, Logic, and Fate Control. I. Wait-time." *Journal of Research in Science Teaching*, 11(2): 81–94.

——— 1974b. "Reflections on Wait-time: Some Methodological Questions." *Journal of Research in Science Teaching*, 11(3): 263–79.

Rowell, Richard M. 1978. "Concept Mapping: Evaluation of Children's Science Concepts Following Audio-tutorial Instruction." PhD thesis, Cornell University.

Schwab, J. 1973. "The Practical 3: Translation into Curriculum." *School Review*, 81(4): 501–22.

Sesnowitz, Michael, Kenneth Bernhardt, and D. Matthew Knain. 1982. "An Analysis of the Impact of Commercial Test Preparation Courses on SAT Scores." *American Educational Research Journal*, 19(3): 429–41.

Simon, H. A. 1974. "How Big is a Chunk?" *Science*, 183: 482–8.

Stewart, James, Judith VanKirk, and Richard Rowell. 1979. "Concept Maps: A Tool for Use in Biology Teaching." *American Biology Teacher*, 41(3): 171–5.

Symington, David, and Joseph D. Novak. 1982. "Teaching Children How to Learn." *Educational Magazine*, 39(5): 13–16.

Thorsland, Martin N. 1971. "Formative Evaluation in an Audio-tutorial Physics Course with Emphasis on Intuitive and Analytic Problem Solving Approaches." PhD thesis, Cornell Univesity.

Toulmin, Stephen. 1972. *Human Understanding, Vol. 1: The Collective Use and Evolution of Concepts*. Princeton, N.J.: Princeton University Press.

Waterman, Margaret A., and Jane F. Rissler. 1982. "Systematic Study of

Scientific Literature Emphasizing Higher Cognitive Skills." *Journal of College Science Teaching,* 11:336–40.

Watson, James D. 1968. *The Double Helix.* New York: New American Library.

Wiener, Norbert. 1954. *The Human Use of Human Beings,* 2nd ed. New York: Doubleday.

INDEX

Achterberg, Cheryl, 116f
audio-tutorial instruction, 86–7, 138
Ausubel, David P., 122, 152, 154, 171; cognitive learning theory, 12, 40, 70, 97–105; meaningful learning, 7

Benbow, C. P., and J. C. Stanley, 161
Bloom, Benjamin S., 6, 23, 86n, 113, 172
Bogden, Christopher, 9
Brown, H. I., 139
Buchweitz, Bernardo, 74, 89, 90–1

Cardemone, Peter, 9
children, acquisition of concepts, 94–5; activities for concept mapping, 24–8; examples of concept maps, 41, 106, 124, 176, 177, 178
Chen, Hai Hsia, 74, 89–90, 186
chunking, 67–9, 78n
cognitive map, 138–9
concept, 6, 41, 71; defined, 4–5; differentiation, 99–103, 104; introducing with mapping: grades 1–3, 24–8; grades 3–7, 29–31; grades 7–college, 32–4; introducing with Vee, 60
concept mapping (see also concept maps, hierarchical structure), alternative representational forms, 36–7, 39; as evaluative tool, 93–108, 138–40; to foster creativity, 17, 104–5; for interviewing, 122–4; introducing concept maps: grades 1–3, 24–8; grades 3–7, 29–31; grades 7–college, 32–4; nature and uses of, 15–24; as notes-taking tool, 49, 53; vs. outlining, 78, 82–3; in planning curricula, 77–87; in planning a

paper, 49, 52–4; as preinstructional tool, 41–8; propositions, 15–20, 34, 36; redrawing, 35–6; related to road maps, 42–3; scoring, 28, 36f, 37f, 105, 107–8; use of arrows, 35, 38
concept maps (see also concept mapping), 14, EXAMPLES: art, 182; history, 41, 84–5; knowledge, 2; literature, 47, 182; marketing, 170; math, 102, 179; music, 147, 148; planning instructional program, 79; religion, 123; "rubber map," 18; science: 21; (biology) 46, 58, 176(A), 177(D); (ecology) 22, 52, 122, 124; (genetics) 80–1; (meat science) 38; (nutrition) 180; (social science) 108, 178; (water) 16, 176(B), 177(C), 181; sports, 44–5, 50–1, 106
concept propositional analysis, 140–3
creativity, 17, 63, 88, 104
curriculum, 6; example: wastewater project, 83, 86–7; planning: use of concept maps, 77–87; use of Vees, 59, 88–91, 117, 164
cycle diagrams, 37, 39

Dewey, John, 117
Donaldson, Margaret, 120, 137

Easley, J. A., 95
Ebbinghaus, Hermann, 8–9
educating, defined, 5; four commonplaces, 6–7; honesty and responsibility, 9–11
evaluation (see also scoring), construct validity, 105; use of concept maps, 93–

197

Index

Oram, Raymond, Paul Hummer, and
  Robert Smoot, 80
outlines, 78, 82–3

Perry, William, 138
Piaget, Jean, 23, 154, 156, 170–71; interviews, 119–21f; reasoning categories,
  137, 144, 147
Posner, George, 95
Postlethwait, S., J. Novak, and H. Murray, 86
predicability trees, 37, 39
progressive differentiation, defined, 97;
  explained, 99–103
propositions, 15–20, 34, 36, 124–25

record(s) 5–6, 10, 55–6, 69, 60–2, 68; for
  research projects, 161, 164–6; transformation, 61–3, 64f, 65f, 68, 69f, 71,
  166–71
research, educational, 149–51; creating
  educational events, 157–61; data gathering, 161–6; data transformation,
  166–71; knowledge and value claims,
  171–4; proposals, 154–5; sample
  forms, 188–9; selecting a problem,
  155–7; theory-driven, 151–4
Ripple, R., and V. Rockcastle, 120
Rodgers, Joann, 70
Rorty, Richard, 111
Rowe, Mary Budd, 131
Rowell, Richard, 95, 96, 138

Schwab, J., 6, 22, 59
scoring, of concept maps, 36f, 37f, 105,
  107–8; of Vees, 70–2, 118
Simon, H., 78n
socratic teaching, 129–30
statistical methods, 168
Stewart, James, J. Van Kirk, and R.
  Rowell, 99n

subsumption, 101; defined, 97
superordinate-subordinate, 16, 35, 41
Symington, David, and Joseph D. Novak, 9

teaching, 6, 160
thinking and doing, 114–17
"thinking, feeling, acting," 6–7
Thorsland, Martin, 165f
Toulmin, Stephen, 139

value, 157; claims, 66, 73, 173–74; and
  evaluation, 109–13
Vee diagrams (see also Vee heuristic),
  EXAMPLES: art, 185; curriculum, 164;
  definitions, 56; format (simple), 3, 56,
  143, (complex) 150; four commonplaces, 160, 162–63, 164, 165; governance, 165; history, 185; learning, 162–3;
  marketing, 183; parade of Vees, 152–3;
  sciences: 61, 63, 186, (biology) 115, 187,
  (matter) 145, 146, (nutrition) 116,
  (physics) 90; social sciences, 68; teaching, 160, 184
Vee heuristic (see also knowledge claims,
  objects, records, Vee diagrams), 1,
  5–6, 55–9, 150–2; applied to reading
  material, 72–3; defined, 55; and evaluation, 111–18; in instructional planning,
  74–5, 88–91; introducing to students,
  59–66; in research projects, 154–55,
  159–60, 162–5; principles and theories,
  63–6, 71; scoring, 70–2, 118; value
  claims, 66
Volmink, John, 11, 179

Waterman, Margaret, and Jane Rissler,
  73
Watson, James, 88
Whitehead, Alfred North, 1
Wiener, Norbert, 154